A HERO IS MORE THAN JUST A SANDWICH

A HERO IS MORE THAN JUST A SANDWICH

How to Give Up Junk Food Love and
Find a Naturally Sweet Man

Sonya Friedman

G. P. PUTNAM'S SONS / NEW YORK

G. P. Putnam's Sons
Publishers Since 1838
200 Madison Avenue
New York, NY 10016

Designed by Rhea Braunstein

Library of Congress Cataloging-in-Publication Data

Friedman, Sonya.
A hero is more than just a sandwich.

1. Marriage—United States. 2. Interpersonal
relations. 3. Love. I. Title.
HQ734.F766   1986   646.7'8   86-91512
ISBN 0-399-13204-X

Printed in the United States of America
1   2   3   4   5   6   7   8   9   10

ACKNOWLEDGMENTS

TO: Connie deSwaan, my collaborator, whose delicious literary style is responsible for the flavor of this book

TO: Chris Schillig, my editor, whose warmth and patience pulled me through some difficult moments

TO: Michael Stein, Aaron Priest, the Reverend Jack Boland and Dave Bell, whose support and encouragement have sweetened my life immeasurably

And to my newest friend
  Dr. Joseph B. Kiel—my father

Thank You

*Dedicated to the recognition that loving relations don't just happen—
they take hard work on a daily basis by two caring people who are
mature enough to want the best for themselves and each other. And it's
never too late to start.*

CONTENTS

It's a funny thing about life. If you refuse to
accept anything but the best, you very often get it.

—SOMERSET MAUGHAM

Why Didn't Anyone Tell Me?

WHEN I married, I wanted my husband to be the perfect man. He'd be my lover, friend, protector, father, provider of security and adventure, a *Hero*—a man with remarkable strengths, few faults and few frailties, a man with direction, ambition, dazzle, the giver of worlds. When I married Steve, I thought he was the right man for me because I expected him to fulfill those fantasies. Years later, it was clear that he could not be everything to me and I wondered if I'd made the right choice after all. I noticed that other men were more ambitious, nattier dressers; they were the men who *made* the news, instead of just reading it at the kitchen table. I was like many other women in believing that life would be miraculous and blissful if I "got" the right man and he made it so.

It took many years of marriage and self-analysis for me to finally understand that I *had* married the right man, even though "miracles" and "bliss" weren't always happening. What I had to "get" was a grip on the real values of life. I'd been looking for the wrong qualities to define the man I wanted to love and whom I wanted to love me. Like a lot of women, I felt fulfillment was a matter of "getting a man." I didn't really think about *loving* a good man. I'd been taught and was following a set of false standards. And following those standards, I couldn't see that the wrong man wasn't going to give me the right things—now or ever. For too long, I believed that the most sought-after men—the dazzlers, the charmers, the "stars" — were the ones who would provide a stable, loving, safe but exciting environment where I could grow and grow up.

When there are stars before your eyes, they tend to blur the view. Somehow, I lost sight of the human qualities that matter, that endure. Steve was someone with high values, with integrity, and I was lucky that he stuck with me when I went through the stages of doubting him. He gave me stability and confidence that kept me out of the trouble I see my friends and patients getting into—looking for Junk Food Heroes and getting hurt. Junk Food Heroes are men who look "de-

licious and nutritious," but after we open the package—
look below the surface—we discover that what's inside
isn't really right for us. Like the proverbial eater of a
Chinese meal, we devour Junk Food Heroes and then
discover soon after that we're still hungry for love.

Why do we fall for Junk Food Heroes? When we're
unsure of ourselves, we choose our relationships out
of neediness. We seek people to fill the empty spaces
that exist inside us, to make us feel like whole people.
When decisions about love are made from a position
of weakness, not strength, they tend to be the wrong
decisions. We choose the wrong man and try to patch
up unrewarding relationships. They often get progressively worse.

Many women share this story. What we have in
common is that we hope a man will change to suit us.
Even if we know he's a Junk Food Hero, somehow we
expect that marriage will transform his character. If
he's authoritative, he'll mellow; if he's irresponsible,
he'll settle down; if he's elusive and secretive, he'll be
revealing and vulnerable; if he's contentious, he'll be
fair and good-humored. But most of all, by hope possessed, we think that proximity is the real motivator,
that if we live as his wife, he'll know how wonderful
we are, apologize and go on to build our dreams for
us. Be the Hero. We want this to be so.

My friend Ann made exactly this mistake. She finally ended a five-year affair with a Junk Food Hero—a "Shark"—a slick, attractive man with glamor and connections, a man who sold himself for more than he was worth, a wheeler-dealer. For five years John led her on, proclaiming his love on Friday night, proposing on Saturday morning and developing amnesia about marriage plans by Sunday afternoon. They broke up regularly, then reunited. He described the diamond he had in mind for her and told her she was the real jewel in his life. For five years, she jumped when he called and cried when she displeased him, and he manipulated her personality like a master mind-bender. She was fifty years old when she finally said goodbye to him for the last time, suffering through a long mourning period for "the love of her life." What did she lose, really? John was another version of her ex-husband, and she was determined to win this time. She wanted to prove to the world that she could compete for and win the man she thought every woman wanted and every man envied. When she finally agreed to give him up in mind and spirit, quite by accident she met a man who wanted to share his life with her. "I have never been so loved in my life," she told me. To hear her speak this way at fifty-one years of age gives us all hope.

Give up the source of unhappiness, even if it comes

packaged like one thousand earthly delights, and life will change for you. The more you depend on Junk Food Heroes to give you your life, to make the universe happen for you, as Ann did, the less chance you will have to know yourself and your own capabilities. In truth, everyone is an addition to your life—and each addition should be enriching, important or profound. You cheat yourself when you stuff yourself with junk food fantasies. *The more you are, the less you need*—and the more you can let the secure and loving men into your life. The men who can enhance what you already have. The *real* heroes, the sweet guys, are out there for you, but you have to be receptive to them. You must develop a *taste* for them.

Who are they? They aren't the men who demand to be center stage in their lives and yours. The real heroes are the nice guys—men who are naturally comfortable with who they are, who can be giving and vulnerable. They want to share your life, not consume it. They're the men you select on the basis of content, not packaging.

Women easily put themselves into the hands of men who they think will have the same desires for them as they have for themselves—the Junk Food Heroes. Over time, the hidden agenda makes itself apparent—he doesn't have your best interest in mind at all.

When a woman puts her life in someone else's hands,

she loses control of it. Your life is yours. Don't give it away too easily or too cheaply. If someone offers you the experience of a lifetime, be sure it's being engineered by a thoughtful, caring, nice guy, not a man in search of a headline, operating on Junk Food philosophies.

Junk Food Heroes are *addictive*. It's easy to be tantalized and surrender to what looks appealing. By comparison, the nice guys may pale. Bring them closer! Dare to stand them side by side with Junk Food Heroes and list what each one brings to your life. Does the Junk Food Hero look wonderful? Does he make you feel wonderful? Does he frustrate you, hurt you and drive you to more junk food so your health suffers and your hips widen? What of the sweet guy? Can you rely on him to be there when you need him? Is he interested in you? Does *he* frustrate you and drive you to junk food? There will be times when he *will* let you down— he's imperfect—but those times will be far, far fewer than they will be if you choose the elusive Junk Food Hero. The nice guy wants the best for you. Can you give him a chance?

I repeat: Your life is yours. Don't give it away too easily or too cheaply. I have felt strongly over the years that far too many women come to appreciate the true qualities of love only after they get a man and realize they have sold themselves short. I was interested in how women feel that they have grown in the process of recognizing love, so I posed the question to readers in my column in *Ladies Home Journal*. I asked readers to tell me: What's love to you, and what would you do differently the second time around? Hundreds of women responded with touching, funny, poignant, sad and wise comments. Standards change between first and second marriages, from one committed relationship to the next. You'll see a trend in the following responses that reflects a change in expectations after the first time around. Would these answers be yours?

- Someone asked me to marry him. If I had looked at all, I would have had time to think. I did neither. I just had a wedding.
- I wanted sex, good looks, cool!
- I wanted a man who was a good dancer, who was handsome, who would marry me, since I had little confidence.
- I mistook good sex for love.
- Looking back, I see I was escaping from my home.
- Romance.
- I married a man I knew would be a good provider, not a good lover.

In all, about 90 percent of the women who responded listed these reasons for marrying the first time: being taken care of, someone who'd make them happy, sex, looks, stability. The key issue was security or rescue by a man—or a combination of the two.

What did they learn about love? What did they think it was and what did they think it would provide? For the most part, the respondents had matured with the experience of marriage, by building a home, caring for a family and dealing with the vicissitudes of life. Women who thought good sex *was* love came to realize that relationships are made standing up, not lying down. Those who wanted to be taken care of achieved maturity when they could acknowledge their partner's needs, while others took a step backward by equating love with sacrifice—"Love is always putting someone else's needs before your own."

Many women offered wise advice that I pass on to you.

• Avoid men who say, "I don't want marriage and children." They mean it.

• Don't involve yourself with someone who's in a relationship. You'll always wonder if he'll do the same to you.

• Evaluate your relationship with a man as if you were starting a new friendship with a woman.

• If he treats his ex-wife and children badly, eventually he'll do the same to you. Don't make the mistake of thinking it will be different.

• Don't want love so much that anyone will do.

• When you live for someone else, you're asking for trouble.

• Nothing is forever.

Ask these questions before going into a relationship.

• Who is responsible for your identity, well-being and life's goals? A good answer is "Myself." Look out if you say, "My husband."

• Do you have a good time by yourself? A good answer is "Yes." Look out if you need him to have a good time.

• Do you admire and respect this man? A good answer is "Yes." Look out if the answer is "I will when I get through with him."

• Do you admire and respect yourself? A good answer is "Yes." Look out if you need his admiration and respect before you can give that answer.

• Does he admire and respect me? A good answer is "Yes." Look out if the answer is "He will if I show him what a wonderful wife I'll be."

• Do you like touching him and being touched by him? A good answer is "Yes." Look out if it's "Not especially."

If your experience with love has been problematic because of your choice of men, this book is for you. It will help you clarify what you believe about love—and explain why faulty definitions of it sabotage your chances of finding true satisfaction within a deep, continuing relationship. Chapter 2, Junk Food Heroes, describes the types of men who most tantalize us and who get us into trouble. You've met them all—now learn to resist them.

Hungry For Love touches on the fatal flaws that bring you back to the same wrong types of men again and again—and tells you how to break the habit. Getting the Crumbs Out of Bed dusts off a few myths about love and marriage and helps you understand how to connect with the nice guys, not the Junk Food Heroes. From Cream Puff to Tart takes you to the office, were many women sacrifice love by building an altar to work—becoming tough themselves, a version of the Junk Food Hero. The final chapter asks you to live your life as fully as you can, as joyously as you can, so you will be able to look back and say, "I was the best I could be and I have, Finally . . . No Regrets."

When you have finished reading this book you won't be able to say, "Why didn't anyone tell me" ever again. I'm going to tell you, over and over again. Let us not select our men by their aromatic, mouth-watering, delicious-appearing qualities. Stop and read their labels.

Listen to what others say about them. Look at their relationships. Remember this warning: JUNK FOOD HEROES ARE INJURIOUS TO YOUR MENTAL HEALTH.

Let's begin by looking at the fascinating subject of love and how we acquire our particular taste for it.

1

Love Is an Acquired Taste

MARRIAGE took it on the chin during the volatile seventies, and many couples hit the mat, stunned. Rarely in the history of the civilized world has marriage been so widely perceived as being tantamount to voluntary incarceration. Marriage was scrutinized and found to be a peculiar phenomenon, like a cult—one you wouldn't want to join. Over the years, countless Hollywood or fairy-tale endings had taught us that "happily ever after" meant two impassioned heterosexual individuals, with minds and hearts bound by law, wrapped in love, walking down the aisle hand in hand, seeking their destinies together. The sun shone on the couple that fateful day—figuratively, if not literally—and for a moment all witnesses to the ceremony felt joy for them, touched by their hope, and did not say what they might have been thinking: "May you be the lucky ones among us and stay happily married." In the seventies "Happily ever after" was as likely to refer to partners going their separate ways after a divorce.

The seventies was a decade of astonishing changes. Along with discovering the power of their own assertiveness, ambition and self-hood, many women also found themselves alone as the 1980s opened another era. That was when marriage took on a new, rosy glow. *Bride's* magazine grew thicker with ads for bridal paraphernalia and fertility drugs. Arcane surgical procedures for embryo transplants almost became routine, like taking antibiotics for flu. Women yearned for families again, yearned to belong to a more protective system, to perpetuate an emotional and biological history, to share the batch of brownies they whipped up late one night.

So marriage was okay again, but we still weren't sure if *we* were. Many of us delayed the decision, but eventually followed a course our older sisters or mothers might have taken decades before—we married just to be married, then resented the man for not being who we wished he was. Others, moved by the passion of the moment, married the man who promised us freedom from the working world. Careers were dropped and we assumed traditional roles, the very ones we had rejected ten years before. Once again, we achieved vicariously through our men. And some of us, seeking the perfect, balanced partnership in the two-career couple, found that the balance tended to tip in a husband's favor.

But marriage was supposed to *work* now. It was time. Didn't we have knowledge of ourselves and experience in the world? Wasn't every problem an acceptable topic for open discussion, making it easier for couples to communicate honestly? Weren't two-career couples more the norm than an idiosyncrasy?

These questions can all be answered unequivocally with a resounding Yes. So why are we back to square one? A study published in the *Journal of Personality and Social Psychology* noted that women may be under a certain pressure to get married, considering it a natural step in their lives *even if they are not suited to it.* The study examined the sense of identity in men and women and how it affected the depth of intimacy in relationships by midlife. The conclusion showed "a relation between ego identity and the achievement of intimacy, a relation that differs between men and women. Whereas men who lack a well-developed sense of identity in young adulthood are likely to remain single into midlife, for women, the decision to marry is independent of their achievement of identity."

So basically, we go into marriage with a taste for it. If it sours for us, we're not sure where it started going bad. Besides, we believe that analyzing love takes away from the romance of it. So whatever it was that caused love to die, we'll just hope for a better experience next time. By midlife, many of us are out there searching for love again—the divorce rate, after all, gives us a dizzyingly unpleasant picture of discontent among married couples. If we've taken care of ourselves and allowed ourselves to grow, we've developed a stronger identity and greater self-respect. Our tastes have changed, we hope for the better. Some of us have even achieved astonishing things—made headlines, become courageous, become heroines in our own lives—but our gourmet palates often taste the bitterness of self-defeat. We may be consumed by thoughts of love and hunger for an ideal marriage, or we may be married but feel unsatisfied. We want love, and we need it! We want others to love us in ways that show us we *are* loved. It doesn't happen.

What's wrong? Why are so many of us suffering over being loved or not being loved? Part of it, I believe, comes from not quite understanding what love is and how it works. Love isn't mystical, magical or always unpredictable. It's not something to be won and then abused, ignored over the years. Love isn't just the sizzle of passion, isolated from the individual and given more power than it deserves. Love needn't be sugar-coated to have sweetness or chocolate-covered to be seen as a gift.

Love, when you acquire a taste for the real thing, is one of the great achievements of the human spirit. Unfortunately, the real thing can get lost among fattier morsels, and what passes for love often isn't love at all. Mature love is love between equals—a combination of friendship and affection. It offers a sense of stability and security. It makes you feel better because of the presence of the other. *It is reciprocal!*

Many women don't really love the man as much as they love the idea of having a man in a continuing relationship, or marriage. Others love the things a man can provide, things they then needn't worry about providing for themselves—from basic survival to eye-popping status. Still other concepts of love depend on mythologies about the package love comes in.

Too many of us have given up content for glitz, salesmanship, creative mind-bending. We've forgotten the ingredients that go into making up character, real friendship, long-term connection—what *matters*. Unfortunately the junk food qualities we buy at high emotional prices appeal to the senses. Perhaps we also imbue a man with qualities he may not have and construct fantasies about him. It's junk food love—fancy packaging, little content. He makes you salivate, triggers your cravings. You just can't seem to get your fill. While he appears delicious, he'll starve you. He just can't meet your minimum daily requirement for love.

Your real hero is a naturally sweet man. One of the good guys.

The good guy tells you who he is and he demonstrates it by his behavior. He doesn't sell himself as foie gras and turn out to be a baloney pâté. The good guy is neither a frog nor a prince. He doesn't need a screen test or the cover of *Time* magazine; nor will he spend his days strolling Skid Row, eyes unfocused, all reasoning power burned to a cinder from drugs or alcohol.

The hero is someone we need to develop a taste for. Our tastebuds are jaded. In *Growing Up at 37,* Jerry Rubin wrote, "More pain goes down in the name of love than any other human emotion. I have treated my friends with more care than I have often treated the women I was in love with. I do not expect my friends to be a certain way, but I have huge expectations of my lovers. . . . A friend remarked to me the other day that he was searching for the perfect woman. I told him that the perfect woman already exists—inside him. Love is not finding the right person. Love is being the right person."

This is a lesson that many, many of the women I

see as patients must learn. Here are four of their stories that show what happens when women persist in trying to find the right person and forget about being the right person. The stories tell us about our illusions in love and the reality.

Four Love Stories

Karen's Illusion: Love Means Putting Your Life in Someone Else's Hands

Karen married Ed when she was nineteen and he, at twenty-two, was the paradigm of macho. He played the unattainable male to her worshipful female.

Sexually demanding, controlling and high-powered, he was everything she wanted. If he treated her unkindly, she blamed herself. Karen identified with Ed's view of women—they were inferior, silly creatures, incapable of decisive action. Ed could do no wrong—she even liked his rough style of love-making. Lack of kindness, condescension and demanding sex, Karen thought, added up to *real* masculinity and for twenty years, she thought her marriage was properly balanced.

From the beginning Karen's mother warned her not to marry Ed, because of a story Karen reported after their first date. It was a hot July evening and Karen wore sandals. Ed looked her over and warned, "Never wear sandals with me again." And Karen didn't. Then Ed ordered dinner for them. Steak for him, hamburger for her. "As it begins, so it will end," her mother told Karen ominously. Twenty years later, Ed came home from work late, and made a brief announcement: "I'm in love with someone else. I'm leaving you."

Over the years, Karen was guided and tended by Ed. Her opinions were his, her values were his, her money was his. He was always right in what he did or thought, even when he was proven wrong. Karen excused his unkindness, saying, "Oh, that's just Ed!" But she could find no excuse for his leaving. Her sense of self-esteem plummeted.

Karen had never been very interested in a career, which was one of the reasons she married so young. "Ed was supposed to save me from being an old maid, and from having to work." Karen's opinions about working women were consistent with her conservative views about male and female roles—men conquered the world, women conquered men's affections; men aspired, women did housework; men were abusive, women excused them. It was 1980 and she had to re-evaluate her philosophies and join the modern world if she was to save herself.

Then she met Bob and had a tempestuous affair with him over the next few years. Bob was more *stylishly* macho than her ex-husband, but an equally lethal character to a woman like Karen. Bob was less attainable than Ed, divorced and not interested in making Karen his second wife. In his approach, though, he told a different story—he offered Karen the moon if she'd just have patience. Four years later, he was still suggesting marriage, but he was never ready to set a date or make the announcement official. Bob was a tempter—all seduction and empty promises, an exploiter, a man who loved being adored. Realizing he'd never marry her, Karen left him, but took with her dreams of a passionate reconciliation.

It never happened. Instead, she turned to Vic. Vic is terrific, although some might call him average. He loves Karen and is good to her. Vic has none of Ed's overwhelming masculine presence or Bob's dazzle. He gives where it counts. He fulfills Karen's needs—he's there for her. In her heart Karen questions Vic's love and attention—does she really deserve him? What will happen to her with a comfortable kind of love given generously? Will she lose her fatal attraction to dynamic types like Bob? Can she find happiness with someone who's willing to be as much in love with her as she is with him?

It will depend upon Karen's ability to see herself as worthy of love. It will mean giving up the idea that a man who treats her badly recognizes that's all that she deserves. For Karen, as for many other women, it will mean becoming more so that she needs less from another, while not settling for less than a peer relationship. *Love isn't asking someone to save you from experiencing life.*

Lorna's Illusion: Love Means Holding Back Those Parts of You that May Not Be Acceptable

Lorna knows a hundred women like Karen and has nothing but contempt for them. She could never understand Karen's essential passivity, and Karen would be equally baffled by Lorna's aggressive ethic. Lorna insists on controlling everything herself because she is so desperately afraid of having others seize control of her life. Karen wanted to surrender herself to a man, give her life up to someone else so that she didn't have to make decisions. Lorna wants to do it all herself.

Lorna was taught from an early age that a man was who he became and a woman was who she married, and she fully believed in this myth. As she saw it, that was the way of the world so far and in 1955, a woman did her best to choose a man who'd make history *for* her. Lorna was eighteen when she married a man ten years older, a personable young lawyer ready to open a practice who fit perfectly into her dream picture of the future. Frank would fulfill her ambitions and give her what she wanted most—status, privilege and large quantities of money and worldly goods.

Eight years into the marriage, Lorna realized she'd chosen wrong. Frank was restrictive, controlling, a very modest spender. More disappointing was the discovery that her ambition for him exceeded his own—he was happy being a small-town attorney, often taking on small cases for little or no money. Lorna wanted him to specialize in the more lucrative fields of corporate or matrimonial law. At twenty-eight, with two small children, Lorna divorced Frank and took a job as a real estate clerk. Two years later, she met Joe. He was a tall, burly man Lorna's age. Basically shy, he was still recovering from desertion by his wife, who'd taken the children and run off with another man. The three-bedroom house was too big for him to live in alone and he decided to put it up for sale. When she met him at the real estate office, Lorna had other ideas. Joe was Frank's polar opposite—a self-made man, a high-school drop-out from a large family who'd opened a small chain of successful stores across the state. Joe had a basic sweetness to him, a passivity with women that belied his business drive. He was smitten by Lorna, who doted on him, entertained him with her generally ebullient personality and married him six months after their first meeting.

They had been married about four years when Lorna's sister decided to open a small advertising agency. Lorna was bored at home so she took a part-time position there, learning all phases of the business. She soon discovered her natural business ability. She had flair, creativity and talent for bringing in clients. She became a partner and the agency flourished. By age thirty-eight, she was almost a millionaire due to the growth of her business and smart investments.

At first, it was difficult for Lorna to face her ambitions squarely. She was like the vast number of women who marry men whom they expect to succeed for them. She'd been raised on theories that clearly defined certain behaviors as "unfeminine" or "unseemly" or "inappropriate"—and succeeding in business was all of these things. As her agency grew, she claimed greater power in the community and at home, but she went through a period of extreme indecisiveness because she felt she had to make a choice. She could back down and let her sister take on another partner, allowing her husband to maintain his position as chief income producer, or she could enjoy her achievements and let Joe deal with her new persona. At first, it mattered to her what people might think, but Lorna was no fool.

She held on to her business while Joe struggled with her success and popularity.

After twelve years of marriage, her career was on the ascent, while Joe's business had collapsed from a combination of mismanagement and employee embezzlement. Joe was despondent, confused and incapable of dealing with the loss. After a year, he still hadn't made an effort to start again. Lorna had an affair. Joe moved out of their bedroom into a small guest room in the basement. Lorna had another affair. Joe took a job with an old friend in another city and left Lorna, agreeing to divorce only if she settled by giving him a quarter of a million dollars. Her lawyer shaved the sum down by 20 percent, and once again Lorna set out on her quest for the man who'd give her everything.

This time it was Harry, a charming, twice-divorced man who owned a thriving used-car dealership. Their marriage lasted six months. Harry's sexuality knew few boundaries and little censorship, and included repeated passes at her two daughters. Now a three-time divorcée, Lorna believed she'd never marry again. But after a year she met Peter, a professor at a local law school, fluent in a number of languages and happy for Lorna's financial solvency. Peter had always wanted to live well and Lorna, ambitious, attractive and never more sure of herself, was happy to share her life with him. Lorna pretty much pays the way and it doesn't bother either of them. They've made a deal that suits them both.

Marriage gives Lorna a patina of correctness and tradition, and having a man both softens and takes the edge off her heady ambition. She's rich and powerful, but now in her forties, she has no need to marry a man who's equal to her in these ways. It has become abundantly clear over the years that she wants to be in control, though she's willing to publicly defer to her men, tout their glories, appear girlish and a bit helpless. The act fools no one, but everyone understands. Fortunately for Lorna, she too accepts the ambitious side of her nature. It took her three marriages to discover that *love does not mean pretending.*

Ann's Illusion: Love Can Repair All Wounds

Ann was the oldest of seven children. Her family was poor and Ann was expected to help take care of the younger children without complaint. Until she was twenty-two, the year she met and married Bill, Ann never felt loved by her parents, just used as a commodity, a Cinderella. More than anything, she wanted a home of her own and a man to give her the love and attention she never got. Bill seemed to fulfill the promise. They understood each other.

Bill's father worked on the docks, when he was sober enough to get there; his mother had lost interest in motherhood and marriage when he was four years old. She got on a bus to Florida one day and started a new life, refusing contact with Bill over the years. Some finer instinct drove Bill toward the most traditional values and sincere religiosity—it all made sense to him. Ann was perfect as his wife. Though her family was intact as his was not, the household Ann grew up in was disrupted and chaotic, with both parents short-tempered and habitually feeling put upon. Ann was virtually ignored, as Bill had been ignored, but together they would finally know love.

Ann decided she'd keep her factory job for a few more years until they were ready to start a family. Bill agreed. When she was twenty-four one of the foremen took a liking to her, and they began an innocent flirtation. After six months the foreman wasn't satisfied with smiles and charming chatter—he asked to see her after work. Ann declined. The man pressed. She refused again, but this time they were in a narrow hallway with no one around and the man kissed her. Ann knew that if she told Bill, he'd either want to kill her or make it a double homicide. She meant to keep it a secret from him, but the story tumbled from her lips. Bill wanted to know all the details—how long the man had been harassing her, why she encouraged it, why she didn't tell him earlier and whether she really wanted to have an affair. She feared his anger, but he contained himself and wouldn't speak to her for a week. At the end of that time, he demanded she quit her job and stay home.

This accidental kiss set Bill off. His early life flew before his eyes in pictures—his father, wrecked by alcohol, never able to deal with his mother's abandonment. Himself, untended as a child, improvising, learning how to charm friends and their parents so he'd be asked to stay for dinner or longer. That kiss terrified him. Would Ann leave him? Was he unlovable, unworthy?

The kiss frightened Ann too. Part of her had known the foreman had an affair in mind, even though both of them were married, yet she responded girlishly, brightly to his attentions. It would have been easy to have cut it dead right from the beginning. And it had nothing to do with Bill being anything but a perfect husband and lover. The foreman was an older man, handsome in a rugged way. She was young and she liked testing her ability to attract men, though she'd never have committed adultery. She hadn't counted on the foreman being so aggressive. But another part of her—the part that let it happen—reasoned: *It happened and I had nothing to do with it.* That part of her told Bill. Such reasoning easily absolved her, she thought. And why not?

Her parents and Bill's father had been victims, she thought, and now the foreman was ruining her life by trying to take advantage of her. Wasn't it true, after all? Ann saw herself as being incapable of having any control in her own affairs. It was for others to change—for the foreman not to be lecherous, for Bill to change jobs so he'd earn enough money and she wouldn't have to work around such intrusive types, and if she let herself really add up the disappointments in her life, for her parents to have given her the money to go to secretarial school or college so she wouldn't have to bear the noise of an assembly-line job, overseen by a dime-store Romeo.

Bill brought with him a standard of male behavior that gave him authority over Ann: "If you love me, you'll do things my way, and I say that you must stay at home since you can't be trusted." That incident at work was the ultimate threat to Bill and to the stability of Ann's marriage. Bill began to drink, not as much as his father but on occasion to the point where it was easy for him to slap Ann if she irritated him. He took on the qualities of a tyrant and she surrendered to him as the wispy, overburdened wife. He became more suspicious, she withdrew. Then Bill sought help.

Ann and Bill both remember talking about how life would be when they got married—it was going to be *different* from what they'd known as children. It was going to be wonderful and calming, tender and loyal, joyful and honest. Unfortunately, the two well-meaning people who made this vow duplicated the parental roles they most resented. They *were* alike, they *did* understand each other, but both were stuck being victims, underdogs. Together, their sense of inadequacy was intensified, not dispelled. They each have to learn to take responsibility for their collective unhappiness.

Anita's Illusion: Love Means Expecting He'll Want More for Me than He Does for Himself

Anita's marriage reflects a more contemporary dilemma, that of the new "team" marriage—the two-career couple. Our mothers were team players too, but they ran only the household while their husbands provided whatever was necessary to keep the home functioning. Women offered consolation, comfort and children, and tried to live the old adage for men: "A man's home is his wife." If our mothers worked, it was most often in support positions—teacher, secretary, clerical workers, bookkeeper. And even if our fathers labored at menial jobs, they were always considered to be the superior partner, the real power behind the team. Even if he was not really the powerful one, it had to look that way.

The new team marriage is the result of two decades of growing opportunity for the striving woman and the male feminist, who's likely to be as proud of his successful wife as the traditional husband was proud of his wife's pecan pie. One kind of team marriage has the best chance of working—two people meet when both have achieved a satisfying measure of success and neither wants the other to make a sacrifice and give up what he or she has accomplished. They may lead parallel lives in two unrelated professions, and enjoy the different interests they bring to the relationship. The key to their harmonious union is a lack of destructive competitiveness.

The new team marriages have worthy intentions, but couples often discover they're keeping separate scorecards. This happened with Anita and Tony, her second husband. When she was twenty-two, Anita married John, a man twelve years older than her. At the time she was gangly, styleless, painfully shy. John felt powerful and experienced with her—he'd found a woman who was vulnerable, who knew little of the world and who'd look to him as the expert. He thought she would work "for the hell of it." Anita took a job with an international banking firm and soon was promoted to a senior position. With success mounting year by year, Anita became more polished and gained confidence— she was now stylishly pulled together, attractive, still a bit shy but charmingly so.

John resented Anita's growth in business, and to demean her, was fond of relating to his friends stories of her ignorance in each of the seven lively arts. John found it shocking that Anita asked about the plots of operas and couldn't remember that Picasso wasn't French. Anita was astonished to realize one morning that her marriage might come to an end, and she began to understand that it would be her who'd go, not John. But until she was forced to make a decision, she just threw herself into her work.

Then the bank hired Tony to oversee Anita's multibillion-dollar department. Tony was her husband's age, tall, charismatic, married for nearly twenty years to his high-school girlfriend. When they had been working together for about a year, Anita and Tony began an affair. He was everything she'd always wanted in a man. He shared her pleasure in the mechanics of banking, he had no elitist veneer and didn't mock her; he was passionate and good-humored, and he promised to take her with him to the top. She felt sad about leaving John. He'd been responsible for getting her to this point in her life. He'd started the mentoring process, encouraging her more like an indulgent father than a full-fledged champion, but it worked out anyway. In spite of John's efforts to keep her a frightened child in a cold, cruel world where only he could protect her, Anita found her way into the warm haven of professional success and the arms of a loving boss.

Tony divorced his wife and he and Anita married.

It looked as if nothing could go wrong for her now. They had been married only a few weeks when corporate headquarters informed them that they couldn't work together—the company had a new nepotism law, and there was no fighting it. One of them would have to leave. Tony told Anita it would have to be her. Reluctantly, she agreed. The bank placed her in another department that only dealt with the fringes of her expertise. She was bored and let Tony know it.

After a few months of extreme unhappiness at work, Anita started looking for a position similar to the one she'd held before her marriage. She found what she was seeking at a rival organization—it was a position, in fact, on the same level as Tony's. Though he claimed he was happy for her, Tony resented her meteoric rise. Dinner conversation became strained because each had to guard professional information that the other might use to unfair advantage.

They have been married two years now, both of them fearing the worst—a divorce. She loves him, but she also wants a career. Anita always believed it would be Tony who'd lead, and she'd follow. As he moved up, she'd move up. They'd be a real team, just the two of them against the world. Neither of them could deal with the true competitive striving they felt toward the other. And neither could have predicted that Anita would equal and probably surpass Tony. He thought he had it over her by a mile. If Anita had realized that love means that each wants the best for himself or herself *and the other,* she could have saved herself a great deal of pain. *Love is not a contest.*

I believe these stories reveal more than just a few details of four complicated lives. They speak to those of us who married and discovered we'd built marriages different from the ones we'd planned. Karen's plaint: "Why wasn't I told that giving in to a master won't make things easy over the long run? It will only make it easy for a man to leave." And Lorna's: "Why didn't they tell me I'd have to do things for myself and not rely on a man to do the giving?" And from Ann: "Why didn't I guess that marriage wouldn't solve all my problems and turn me into someone I wasn't?" And from Anita: "Why didn't I anticipate that the man who wished me success could be the same one who'd resent that success and want to sabotage it?"

Karen, still a romantic, believed in her great, grand passion, the man who'd be her hero, Ed. She was young when she married, and young women often select men who repeat familiar parental styles that unfortunately keep them children. So it was with Karen. She wasn't running away from home when she walked down the aisle with Ed, but she was running away from herself, from having to grow up. She created in Ed a star, a fictionalized hero who had no interest in Karen's needs, just her attention to the details of his life. For nearly twenty years she just sought Ed's approval. Karen liked having life made simple for her. When she was finally obliged to work and be on her own, she was stunned to find that she could live alone and wouldn't perish without Ed's direction. She learned to do things on her own, dethroning the "master" in her life and installing another one—herself.

With Vic, she's experienced the true hero, the good guy, the fair, reasonable individual who's content with himself and has nothing to prove. He just wanted to connect. Karen distrusts this somewhat—she is not accustomed to love without harsh laws, conditions and strategies attached to it. She's attracted to the kindness but misses the *rush* that men like Ed or Bob evoke in her.

Lorna was ambitious at a time when women had little freedom to carve out a career. Instead, women's personal ambitions were directed toward motivating husbands. Success was vicarious, therefore, the more desirable, successful and powerful the man, the greater one's womanly value. Lorna's first husband, the lawyer, had different plans for himself than Lorna had. She wanted status, he chose moderation and charity. He couldn't take care of her in ways that meant something to her.

In Lorna's second marriage, Joe had money but he lost it and never retrieved the confidence to make it again. Lorna might have seen the light then—seen that it was okay to do it herself if another couldn't do it for her—but she snapped it off. Stubbornly, she held on to an ideal that would forever disappoint her. She still yearned to be *given* her dreams. Her third marriage was a foolish episode with an amoral lothario, but she was starting to accept herself as the major income producer in any arrangement she might have. With her fourth husband, she grew into the role of rich entrepreneur and began to enjoy it as Peter found immense pleasure in what money can buy.

As with so many star-crossed lovers, Ann and Bill were fleeing painful, empty home lives and tried to establish a haven of generosity, friendship and gentleness. But they were working with the raw materials of their heritage: What could they do but reconstruct their parents' lives, in a style all their own? Each, half a person, found the other. To their surprise, they remained two unsteady halves, hobbling backward toward history.

Ann carried her mother's fatalism into her marriage, believing that every force in the outside world was too great to challenge, so great that one shouldn't even try. Another side of that fatalism compelled Ann to blame her own motives and actions on others—to believe that things were done *to* her, not *by* her. She couldn't possibly have been leading the foreman on!

Ann wants her life to change, to be different from the unsatisfying one her mother led. But she wants it to change around her, without her having to examine her own inner world and take responsibility for it.

Anita went through a dramatic transformation with both of her men. John established the kind of relationship that felt right to him—a parent-child relationship. Anita, fresh from college, virginal, adored John for his knowledge and attentiveness. At first, working meant little to her because it meant little to her husband. Then she discovered the full extent of her abilities and she could not stop herself, nor did she want to. She thought John would be strong enough to accept her position, her money-making potential, but he wanted the child in her, not the entrepreneur.

Tony promised but he didn't deliver. Anita entered what she thought was a "team" marriage, but it became a competition, a battleground. Tony thought himself the greater of the two—he'd "bring her along." But Anita surpassed what both of them had in mind for her, and not too many men are fully capable of handling career success in a mate—especially when she's in the same business. In fact, some recent studies suggest that the mental health of husbands decreases as they perceive the loss of their sole-wage-earner's role.

Tony loves Anita but he feels betrayed. Anita loves Tony, but feels cheated. This is not the way they thought love would work out for them.

What Is Love and How Does It Grow?

Ask someone newly in love what love is, and the responses will focus on ecstasy, oneness, fullness, "coming home." Speak to someone newly wounded by love, and you will hear about agony, loss, bitterness, confusion. Question a romantic who is on a mission to find the *right* love, and you'll hear stories of rapture, surrender, adventure, conquest. Probe the mind of a cynic who's been deeply hurt at least once and you'll discover theories about the myth of love, about the supremacy of lust or work and how they substitute for connecting to another human being, about how love is a psychic weakener and the heart's main function is to pump blood, not create emotional havoc.

Love will contain most of these elements at some time in our lives if we've opened ourselves to the experience. But all these sensations, from passionate to passionless, are what we may know about love *at first*. They're based on primitive feelings and immediate connections to a fantasy—someone turns us on because he's attractive in a way that matters most to us. Love changes over time, though, because life trickles in, event by event, and dulls the illusion. One wants control, another makes unreasonable or even reasonable demands a partner won't accede to; bills aren't paid, partners each want something different from life and neither will help the other. Tempers flare, jobs are lost or gained; a partner drinks, cheats, cannot be straight and honest. Are you still in love through it all? Mostly, you try to remember the first moments, to recapture the bliss, the high when you first fell in love.

How, in fact, did it happen? Generally, falling in love happens in five distinct stages. The first is *attraction*. This initial magnetism is often based on "chemistry" and fantasy. An interaction occurs between two people that's filled with a sense of potential rewards and pleasure. A woman might, for example, react to a man by saying to herself that he is charming or powerful or influential, or creative or funny, or just interested in her! This is a stage of great passion and high intensity because of the newness of the relationship, the edge of anticipation and the sense of urgency.

Dr. William Glasser wrote in *Reality Therapy* that the faster two people decide to commit, that is, the quicker they fall in love, the harder the impact, the higher the high, the hotter the flame, and the quicker the relationship will ignite and burn off.

This introductory step, which can turn into instant intimacy, gets people into all kinds of trouble. The *attraction* fools us into thinking we've found our match. We've probably all experienced this and experimented with it. And some of us get stuck there, craving newness and overvaluing passion in relationship after relationship.

The next step is *exploration:* A couple are willing to take their time and get a sense of each other in spite of the passion. The question no longer is, Am I ever going to see you again? but, What do we see in each other? What really drew us together beyond physical attractiveness or the fact that one has something the other likes or needs? What do we have in common? Do we have the same sensibilities or interests? Is there a feeling that we're on the same wavelength—or that we have qualities that put us on an equal footing? Do we agree on value and standards? Both will begin to relate their life stories in more vivid detail—the kind of stories that draw the couple closer.

The third step involves *revelation:* A couple now test how much intimate knowledge they can exchange and still feel safe. Can you tell a secret and not worry about being betrayed or humiliated? How does the one you care for feel about certain skeletons in the closet—

your "past"? You become more vulnerable with revelation, and you aren't always on your best behavior. You can scream at your mother, slam down a phone, curse, show an unattractive side, a bad temper, an active bias or hostility, without self-consciousness. This is also when rejection may begin, if one partner reacts badly to what is revealed by the other.

After revelation, there will be a sensitive stage in which doubts arise. This is *ambivalence:* In the revelatory stage, one or both members of the couple may make transparent or even preposterous excuses for inconsiderate behavior. The person on the receiving end may be willing to go along with the deception just to keep the peace, and the relationship. Or you may ask yourself: Do I *want* him? Is he constructing these fables about why be can't see me because he wants to break things off and can't do it honestly? If he wants to break things off, will I get along without him? In fact, do I want to end it first? Or, what's the least I can do to win him back or the most I must do to insure his love?

With the ambivalent stage, you'll waver between wanting to free yourself from your partner one moment and feeling a heavy, urgent and abiding need for him the next. The revelatory stage opened up to you the realness of the man—how he truly copes, what he thinks about money, what he wants from a woman, whether he's reliable, whether he says one thing then goes off and does what he pleases all the time, whether he has personal standards you admire or has set them at so lofty a level that you could never please him.

The ambivalent stage presents you with the challenge of figuring out what you want from this relationship, and whether you want it to go on. If you do, your wounds will heal. You'll understand more about how you and your lover interact at your best and at your worst. But some relationships should end when the basis of exchange is pain, not joy in each other. If the writing's on the wall, remember the good moments and look at what you've learned from the relationship—but be ready to end it.

Everyone experiences ambivalence and doubt. In religious orders, such experiences are a test of faith. Are you called to this vocation or not? The same can be true for getting through this test of caring: Are you willing to commit and can you do so with a pure heart?

Love can't endure on a diet of romantic ideals and won't thrive when one person is in control of defining the terms of the relationship. Love needs maintenance, attention, discussion, scrutiny, adjustments, confrontation. For the final stage—*union*—we need to be kind to ourselves, kind to our partners and willing to look at the quality of our contribution to the relationship. *Love requires work.*

*　　*　　*

We all want love to last, but we may not be giving it the chance it needs. We suffocate it, bend it out of shape, turn it into power plays, or try to squeeze it into self-made molds. Most of all, I think we begin with a faulty idea of what it is in the first place, which creates greater problems than you can imagine. This idea is that somebody is going to do better by us than we could do for ourselves. We are consumed by this idea, and driven by it, we try to find the right person to protect us from the real world, read our minds, know what we want and give it to us in exactly the form we want it in.

When you center everything on a love object, he can only do one thing—*fail you*. If he's all there is and you expect him to give you all you want, well, you are building a pedestal to hold a peanut. Whoever the man is—from tycoon to ordinary—he's a guy with flaws. He cannot fulfill your dream, in most cases. At best, he's a man who does the best he can; he's someone who goes out there and *tries*.

What do we want from someone else? This is an important question because the answer is often this: We want more *of* and *from* others than we want from ourselves. We've wasted many years resenting not having what we want, more years absorbed in fantasies about what we're deserving of and how we'd behave if we had what we wanted, and even more years not appreciating *who* we are. We are women who can *do for ourselves* and that's not so terrible. It shouldn't reflect on our personal sense of worth if a man doesn't buy us what we want or make us feel better about ourselves.

Getting what you want for yourself involves hard work, not sitting and pining away for things. It means making an investment in yourself, having the where-withal to enjoy your own company; establishing a net-work of people you can call on, having something outside yourself. You must learn not to depend on another to satisfy your longings.

When you've learned that lesson, you can begin to acquire a taste for real love. What are its ingredients? It's a delicate mix of many things.

• You don't need to be self-sacrificing, to surren-der your life to another or keep a running score, but you can give generously, freely and joyfully. I favor psychoanalyst Harry Stack Sullivan's theory that with real love, the needs and satisfactions of another are as important as your own.

• You know you're okay on your own, but you're enhanced by the one you love because he brings out that *okayness* and gives it a special brilliance.

• When you love, you can openly tell another

person that you appreciate him, that you enjoy who he is and happily *invite him into your life*.

• You can plan for a future together and keep a good sense of humor through the setbacks, the trials, the inevitable hard times.

• You have a healthy degree of interdependence, which doesn't mean that you give your life over to a man, but you do feel that you're part of what makes his life click.

• You accept another's idiosyncrasies and don't demand change.

• After the rush of early passion, you can sustain a level of pleasure and acceptance of yourself and the other person. To keep the relationship worthwhile, you establish goals. You both know what you want over the long run.

• During courtship, you're not "yes men" to each other, smoothing over the rough spots with flattery, false excuses, delusions. Rather, you use courtship well and wisely. Many promises are made during the initial rush of love—a "divine madness" that has little to do with the reality of maintaining a mature relationship. Don't hesitate to rock the boat by discussing inconsistencies, confusions, hurt feelings.

• You'll be able to get up every day, look at the man you've chosen and say to him, "Today I voluntarily commit myself to the relationship," or the marriage.

If the words catch in your throat, taste stale or un-palatable, talk it out immediately. If it's love, the response to your doubts should be eager concern. If the response is, "That's your problem," you may have chosen someone who sees the relationship as his and the troubles as yours.

• If you are in love you don't make assumptions. Know the facts—love can endure straight, unromantic information. What plans did you make and expect your mate to carry out? Did he? Could he? What dreams was he to enact for you? Was he meant to be your ideal, the man who'd fill all the roles you needed a man to fill—husband, lover, teacher, father, pal, provider, protector? Did he satisfy those needs or disappoint you? If you assumed wrong, take a look at the man and accept his limitations if you want him.

• In love, your union adds up to three—together you create an entity that's greater than the sum of its parts. You can maintain your uniqueness as individuals, but allow an easy, natural interdependence.

• With love, you know the feeling of being the lover and the beloved—and you may like the active role of lover more than the passive role of the beloved.

Does such a healthy love exist or do its ingredients add up to an unattainable ideal? I think the following story answers that question.

JoAnne came to see me last year and presented a truly fascinating love story. I pass it on to you because I think it exemplifies a mature, giving, exciting, reasonable relationship. JoAnne's story is different from the four discussed earlier in this chapter. Those were about people still struggling with their needs and expecting a false concept of love to satisfy them.

This more nearly ideal union is not without struggles, but it allows JoAnne and Don to continuously and unabashedly scrutinize the relationship, set and meet joint goals and create a tighter bond. This couple were as mesmerized by each other as the others were. But these special two are thinking clearly as they pass through passion and on to the various stages of knowing each other and testing each other.

JoAnne and Don are fifty years old and both are in love, they say, for the first time. When JoAnne was twenty, she married Ken. Then, she'd been intoxicated by a romantic vision of love and of living happily ever after, but things had changed.

When she was forty-five, she left Ken. She felt she had fulfilled the objectives of matrimony—she'd been a good wife and a supportive team member, she'd raised three responsible children and participated well enough in community events. Something snapped when she reached forty, and she could no longer ignore her deep yearning for an intimate relationship. She didn't have it with Ken and she knew that every year with him would be more of the same—barely anything. It took her five years to leave and establish her own life.

Don was from a genteel New England home. He thought he'd be a great American novelist, and he married a woman who believed in him and saw him as a prize, and a prize winner. He cared for Betty and appreciated her support, encouragement and intuitive sense of when to leave him alone, but there was no passion, no fiery enthusiasm. That was okay, he could concentrate on his career.

After twenty-five years of marriage, he had a clean, well-kept, lavish home, healthy, educated children, a position that paid a six-figure income and a feeling of loneliness. His marriage was in the same place it had begun. He and Betty liked and respected each other, but was this all? Don told Betty he wanted to separate for a while—he was restless and didn't want to hurt her, but there was nothing else he could do.

Six months later, JoAnne walked into his life. They met on an assignment and liked each other immediately. Don didn't ask her out, though he wanted to the moment he saw her. It was JoAnne who made the first move, surprising both of them. She approached him in a straightforward manner and told him that she liked him, enjoyed him, desired him, but that she felt vulnerable to him. Don told her that he was still in a long-term relationship, and that he felt affection and loyalty for Betty but yearned for some greater intimacy with a woman.

JoAnne had thought about what she wanted from Don—from any relationship, actually—and from herself. "I told him I'd come out of a marriage where I thought I'd live happily ever after," she told me. "And now, being a lot wiser, I wanted a renewable contract. Don laughed and said he'd sign for the next seventy years. I suggested three months at a time."

They had not even kissed yet.

After three months, she broached the issue of assessing their relationship. Don thought there was nothing to assess, since nothing had gone wrong so far. "I needed to know that he cared for me and if there were aspects of the relationship he didn't like, I wanted to know about them," she told me. "I needed to be nourished—even if it was just a phone call checking in to see that I was okay. I needed to be told I was loved. I'd barely heard it in my marriage and hearing those words mattered to me. I wanted to intensify the commitment and if Don didn't, I had to know now. At three months. If he wanted to go back to Betty, I had to know . . . now. I'd be unhappy about it, but I'd respect his judgment. Even if the result was unhappy for me, I'd still ask for that three-month appraisal.

"We're waiting to get past the point of passion

before we make a decision about the future," says JoAnne. "If this relationship ends, I know we have the basis for a continuing friendship. It was how we began and we've only made it stronger. I don't want to have any regrets. I didn't hold back with Don, and he's been direct with me.

"If we should part, I'll know we did our best—that I never deliberately hurt him, that he never had a need to destroy something in me to make himself feel bigger, stronger, heroic."

JoAnne's relationship with Don has been, if nothing else, a rehearsal for a better one that may eventually materialize for her. She now knows what she wants, and it's her choice to look for it, and if she finds it, to take it into her life.

Not all marriages end in love and not all love ends in marriage. What both can be is a growth experience. Love teaches, if only you will listen. In a relationship, one hopes, you've tuned in to some truths about yourself, how you feel, how you really react to love, to the pressures of a relationship, to demands from others upon you.

The lesson these stories tell us is a simple one, but it's one that's often difficult for us to see in our own lives: Until you know who you are and let others know, you're never going to get what you want. To know who you are, begin by identifying the *patterns* you repeat over and over. Look at whom you seek to give you love. Is it the very person who *cannot?* Perhaps you share some of the tendencies of the four women whose stories were told earlier.

Are you like Karen? Do you want someone who'll take over your life? Does making decisions for yourself scare you?

Are you like Lorna? Do you hide your ambitions and desires from yourself and others? Do you suggest to a man that you believe one thing, while actually believing another? Do you fear your desire for achievement marks you as unfeminine?

Or are you like Ann? Having once been victimized, do you seek out other victims? Do you believe that two wounded halves make a whole? Are you interested in saving a man and being his love nurse?

Or, finally, are you like Anita? Do you compete with men but deny it? Do you want someone to bring you into the world—be your mentor—then seek someone to *give* you the world? Do you feel you have to stunt your emotional and professional growth to have a man in your life?

If you're like any of these women, the chances are good that you may select men as they do, and the men they *do* select are the Junk Food Heroes. They're the men who seem accessible, tantalizing, appealing, easy to take in daily doses. They attract women and fatten them with lies and dreams. They plug in to a woman's weaknesses, promise love and protection but keep her wanting. You've met them. They're men like these . . .

2
Junk Food Heroes

BARBARA was thirty-four when she met Tom—a man ten years older, worldly, ambitious, attractive, divorced and ready to settle down. Though they'd known each other only a few months when they decided to marry, it felt right to both of them. Barbara worshiped Tom and he adored being her god. They agreed on everything, including deferring their "real" honeymoon to sometime in the future in favor of a long weekend at the closest resort they could find.

The first day of their marriage, Barbara said, was *wonderful* until the evening. At dinner Tom appeared restless and agitated and told her he wanted to go out for a walk alone and pick up a pack of cigarettes. He'd meet her back at their room in an hour or so. Barbara lingered over coffee, upset, then began chatting with the couple at the next table to calm down. She went back to their room at the agreed time.

Tom hadn't come back yet. Barbara waited.

Two days later, Barbara's wait was finally over. Tom returned the night they were to drive back to the city. Barbara hadn't left the room in two days, too frightened to bring up the matter of her husband's disappearance with the police and too embarrassed to deal with questions she couldn't answer from hotel staff and guests. But he was back—that was what mattered. And he was very apologetic. "It was marital fright," he told her. "It was crazy of me to leave, but I'll make it up to you." Barbara promised to forget the incident.

Six months into the marriage, Tom dressed for work one morning and announced coolly: "I have to escape from this." Unmoved by her pleas to stay and work things out, Tom left her with this advice: "Do what you have to do."

Barbara did nothing. She waited. One year later, Tom knocked at her door, wanting to come back. He desperately needed her. Thrilled to have him in her arms again, Barbara agreed to start over. Then she discovered part of Tom's need for her: He'd reunited with Tina, an old girlfriend, and run up thirty thousand dollars in bills. Tom spoke to her candidly: He couldn't pay off this big a debt on his salary, so could she kick in some of her earnings, and ask her uncle (for whom he worked) to give him a raise?

Barbara deliberated. Tom wanted her to help pay for entertaining Tina in the last year in ways he had never entertained her. Though her uncle had wanted to fire Tom when he left Barbara, she took his side. Barbara believed Tom would return just as he did the first time, so there was no reason to sabotage his career. Yes, she told Tom. She'd do it. To have him back, she'd do anything. How she loved him!

Barbara was happy enough with Tom over the next few years, even though he appropriated Monday and Tuesday evenings and all day Saturday for himself, refusing to tell her where he went. He denied that he was seeing Tina again.

As her birthday approached this past year, she decided to risk it and ask Tom to spend all day Saturday with her to celebrate. He agreed. But he left at six that Saturday morning, promising to take her out to dinner instead. Then Barbara remembered it was also Tina's birthday and that Tom was probably with her.

Three years of marriage hadn't changed him, but now Barbara knew the union was doomed, altogether intolerable for her. She loved him, craved him and wanted to be married. She hated what was happening, but she couldn't leave. "As long as Tom's married to me, I'm the winner. I only lose if there's a divorce and he's free to go back to Tina or any other woman."

This certainly isn't a traditional love story, but it is a love story nevertheless. Its unique plot describes how one set of lovers love. Though it's a love story, it focuses on emotional cravings, hungers and illusions, not joy, connections, warmth and comfort. In this tale, love doesn't nourish the soul, it wrenches the gut.

Barbara is on a quest for love. More accurately, she is on an ill-conceived and sadly disoriented journey supported by an erroneous idea of what love is and how it should appear, feel and taste. And Tom is the man of Barbara's dreams, her hero. If he's not perfect, well then, at least his shoes are under *her* bed. Twice he's hurt and humiliated her—leaving without explanation, impulsively, selfishly, childishly. He's clearly leading a double life, and with her rival. Yet she stays. Barbara's self-esteem is so low that she'll take what Tom tosses her—the crumbs. This is what he'll give her of himself to feast on. Tom is her Junk Food Hero.

The Makings of a Junk Food Hero

The seven types of men you'll meet later in this chapter, like Tom, qualify as Junk Food Heroes. Like Barbara, you've dated them or loved them at least once, and may have married one. A serious addict, you may even have married one type *more* than once. Who is the Junk Food Hero? The embodiment of the ultimate palate-pleasing sandwich (a "hoagy" in some regions), the Junk Food Hero touts himself as having it all.

The junk food hero—the sandwich—has a reputation in some circles as being the "perfect" food. Layered between two hunks of French bread are a variety of deli meat slices, cheese, the optional onion, shredded lettuce, wheels of tomatoes, anchovies or olives if you want them, a bit of seasoning and thick-spread condiments like mayonnaise and mustard. It offers variety, flavor and a representative from every food group and it doesn't take much culinary skill to stack the ingredients. Its simplicity entices us—even a child can "cook" a hero. Its brother, the sausage hero, is earthier and more colorful with thick, garlicky fried links doused with tomato sauce as sweet and thick as maple syrup, topped with slightly browned onions fresh from crackling on the grill.

The junk food hero can be found anywhere, even at home. It appears to contain every nutrient known to man—protein, carbohydrates, fats, vitamins, minerals, amino acids, and, as an added fillip, a piquant spice. But let's lift off the crunchy top slice of bread and examine the contents more closely. What we're scrutinizing is not all that wholesome. High-fat meats (with sausage, fried in oil), processed cheese, mealy tomatoes, sugar-loaded sauces, salt-laden ingredients on flavorless lids of white bread with the texture and nutritional value of newspaper. A hot fudge sundae is junk food, but at least it's honest! The junk food hero asks you to believe it will not only satiate your hunger but keep you alive—that it's a source of life.

Junk food usually has eye appeal. It's well-packaged and stimulating to the appetite. It evokes an aura of pleasure. It leads us to believe we're getting a lot for the money. Its scent is provocative, its familiarity is comforting and it's always accessible.

And how we crave it. Few of us turn to steamed carrots when we feel lost, unhappy. Fewer seek consolation at a juice bar. And not many sneak bits of rice crackers in the middle of the night to assuage feelings of emptiness. Junk food has a purpose—it comforts the child in us, at least momentarily. Junk food was the reward for being "good" and a way of smoothing hurts and relieving stress when we were children. We've all carried the weight of junk food's deeper meaning into our adult lives. And some of us have cheated ourselves by developing tastes for men who are momentarily as rewarding, warming, sweet, piquant or salty as the junk food of our choice. *They're* the Junk Food Heroes.

The Junk Food Hero, the man, creates as false an impression about himself as does the sandwich. At first, he may appear to have layer upon layer of soul-nourishing qualities, but in truth, he only goes as deep as his own needs. Yet we crave him, and crave him again and again! These Junk Food Heroes aren't the men who are good for us, yet they create a strong gut reaction of desire in us.

Discovering Your Taste in Men

Relationships are as different as the people who contribute to them. Giving, withholding, joyful, sharing, trusting, fearful, passionate, self-indulgent, quieting, controlling—all these are individual qualities that affect a partner and determine whether the relationship will be lasting or temporary, gratifying or rejecting, sweet or bitter.

How we love, at the core, is as essential a statement of who we are as what we do and whether we light up a room or dim the sun. Loving is a willingness to take risks and trust another, rather than backing off and choosing a safe emotional isolation, with or without a partner. How we *think* of love will dictate our choice of a mate, and how we *express* love will keep us with another, fulfilled or confined, satiated or hungry for love.

We grow up with concepts of love that help shape the lover we choose. Most of us have changed our opinion of love more than once, depending on the time of life or the needs of the moment. We've wanted love and acceptance and asked them of someone for whom *giving* is unthinkable. We've been adored by someone who sees the universe in us when all we see in him is *nothing.* How often have you gone to a party knowing for certain that once again you'll seek out a man who'll be seductive, or distant, or overpowering or cowed— the very type that's wrong for you?

How we love and the values that direct our choices in love are complicated matters. An emotionally constructive or destructive childhood shapes our self-images in positive or negative ways. Even if we come from deprived circumstances—emotionally unwholesome or love-barren homes, battlegrounds with angry, bitter, joyless, alcoholic or drug-abusing parents—we can develop self-concepts that are healthier, nonimitative parental models. This miraculously stronger self allows us to lead more fruitful lives and make right choices. But sometimes we get *stuck* over some point in our emotionally deprived past, and we are drawn to certain modes of behavior, attracted to men who are guaranteed to perpetuate what's wrong for us.

Most of all, our understanding or misunderstanding of love emerges from an abundance or lack of caring in childhood. Women who are raised by emotionally generous parents don't fear that love, affection or security will suddenly come to a halt. As children, they called out and their voices were heard; they needed to lean, and there was a shoulder; they felt doubt, there was assurance and encouragement. Such women are the lucky ones. Having experienced a trusting love, one that's always replenished, they're more likely to give emotional sustenance to others. But those women raised with a lack of caring and an abundance of un-pleasantness may find it difficult to share or receive love, too. In the next chapter, Hungry for Love, we'll identify the factors in childhood that influence love choices. Before we do that, let's look at the kinds of Junk Food Hero we are drawn to.

The Salty, Sour Seven: Beware These Junk Food Heroes

Who is the man who represents love for you?

Is he galvanic, commanding, "somebody"? Is it his style that overwhelms you? In a relationship, is he domineering, controlling, a saboteur? Do you think he's Good'N'Plenty, when he's really a *Boss?*

Is he physically dazzling, "delicious," slick, a wheeler-dealer, as likely to call you from a hotel room in Berne, Switzerland, as from Dubuque? In a relationship does he stun you with silence or maim you with convoluted logic or outright lies? Is he a *Shark?*

Is he boyish, lovable, sweet as pie, needy? In a relationship is that sweetness all surface, all wrapping? Underneath, is he unreliable, spoiled, narcissistic, a *Golden Boy?*

Is he strong, reticent but fascinating? In a relationship is he indecisive and critical, afraid of intimacy? Is he a *Shadow?*

Do you know for certain what kind of love you seek? Do you start out wanting one thing and end up with another—always confused, feeling cheated, rejected, unappreciated? Does it seem that your definition of love and your actual experience of relationships will forever be two very different things? Can you be an attentive observer and note your responses to a man you love and how you promote or provoke responses from him?

In this chapter I'll try to help you determine which Junk Food Hero trips you up before going deeper into why. To complicate matters, the upcoming profiles of men (the Boss, the Shark, the Golden Boy, the Shadow and others) may include facets of your own personality and those of your parents. The profiles describe a man's *prevailing* character trait—the one to which you are drawn compellingly and repeatedly. Few Junk Food Heroes exhibit the characteristics of only one of these types, but each overall style suggests who they are and why they cannot provide the wholesome love you seek.

They may be afraid of intimacy, or controlling, verbally abusive, begrudging, cheap. It's the prevailing characteristic of each Junk Food Hero that defines the relationship for you and reveals your attraction and addiction to him.

The Boss: You think he's Good'N'Plenty (sweet and colorful outside with a delicious treat inside), but he's really a jawbreaker (an outsized glob of sugar-coated gum that's more challenge than chomp).

The Shark: He's like Tom, the quintessential Junk Food Hero, the oiliest man alive. Slick and slippery, his layers are many and his superficialities run deep.

The Golden Boy: He's as cute, darling and fragile as a gingerbread boy, but in truth he's an instant soufflé—he demands to be served immediately or he'll leave you flat.

The Shadow: He's white bread—neutral, lacking real flavor and emotional substance.

The Banker: The alter ego of the Shadow, the Banker is white toast—a bit warmer and sweeter, but getting him to part with a dime can turn into a taffy pull.

The Loser: He's stone soup, contributing no flavor to the broth of life.

The Blaster: Alter ego of the Loser, the Blaster is a stone sandwich: bite on this and it'll knock your teeth out!

*　　*　　*

The Boss

Make no mistake: The Boss needs you, but he needs power more. Power means command, control, followers. At his lowest, he's the common bully. At his most evolved stage, the ruthlessly ambitious man, he controls others in more socially attractive ways. He's not domineering, he's "authoritative"; not opinionated, but a "renowned expert"; not tyrannical, but a "born leader."

You couldn't miss him in a crowd. His voice rises above the others, his chin juts proudly, his eyes are clear and purposeful as they sweep the crowd for loyal supporters and worshipful lovers. He expects to find you among them. He wants to marry you.

That's why you're attracted to him. He's decisive, even about long-range plans that include *you*. He impresses you as knowing everything, even if he doesn't. A Boss makes you feel special, cared for, protected, sometimes as his adored little girl. Whether he's an out-of-work actor or a Nobel-prize genius, a shoe salesman or a Supreme-Court-judge-to-be, he looks like a catch, a man with a rosy future.

The Boss has studied marriage, and he wants it *his* way!—an exclusive relationship wherein he excludes you from making decisions. The rules will be his— you'll be monitored and directed, as in, "Where were you? . . . Let me know how much it costs and I'll let you know . . . You're wrong, as usual." His chief role model is Louis XIV, known to have proclaimed, "L'état, c'est moi." His guiding axiom was spoken by James Earl Carter, thirty-ninth American president, who said cheerfully, "Show me a good loser, and I'll show you a loser."

When the Boss marries, his cottage is his state, and he wins every point. Even if, in truth, you've won, you lose. His standards are law, and whether you are a good wife or not depends entirely on his system of measurements and balances, which may fluctuate from day to day. But, he actually likes marriage. He feels safe there. The outside world can be cruel to him. There are always bigger, meaner, shrewder, more controlling Bosses, and he may work for one. In a relationship with a less assertive wife, he gets to live two lives—his and hers. As part of the marriage vow, he expects a woman to surrender her life to him, and he'll run it with a continuing litany of promises and orders. And don't believe that eternal peace in death means release from his control. He'll have a scheme to manipulate your estate or contest your will, and if you stipulated burial spot "X" he'll merrily bury you in spot "Y."

A Boss can be generous. He'll buy you diamond bracelets, ruby rings and pearls from Hong Kong, if he can afford them. If your marriage dissolves, the Boss may hire a lawyer to wrest those pearls from you. His argument: The jewelry wasn't bought as presents for you, but as an investment. Not that he cares about the dollar value of the cache; he just wants his power to empty your dresser drawers to continue after marriage.

He's known to be romantic, boyishly charming, fast and funny. He wants to be loved, adored, agreed with, worshiped—but don't get too close. He cannot live without you, but your ability to make him feel intimidates him. He's basically *very* insecure and feels wretchedly inadequate. His style—all bravado—is designed to fool you and himself. He goes from sweet to sour with the snap of a finger.

The Boss must control himself, then control you. This he does in a number of ways: demeaning comments, interrupting you in the middle of an impassioned speech and changing the subject to something irrelevant; making phone calls, leaving the room or starting a conversation with someone else as you begin to speak; humiliating you in public, encouraging you to perform a task then insisting he has no time to see, hear, or travel to what you've accomplished. To be sure he's in control, he'll create disturbances, cause panic and make threats to let you know—he's the Boss.

Feelings of vulnerability terrify him. Heartbroken, one Boss described the dissolution of his marriage by hitting himself hard on the chest whenever he felt he might cry or display any sign of emotional loss. Another Boss demanded that his wife not move, respond or make a sound while he was having sex with her. She had to accept what he did and show neither pleasure nor displeasure. He feared intimacy to such a paralyzing degree that he needed his wife to behave as if she were, in fact, paralyzed.

If you've lived with a Boss, you've learned that anger is one of his closest friends. It's the one emotion the Boss can fill a room with, vigorously and courageously. Some Bosses will close up, shut down and back off— they're masters of the prolonged silent treatment and other cruel mind games. Others will browbeat, shout or strike out with brutality.

The craving for control or power is not the essential problem. There are people who can control with magnanimity, grace and a sense of fairness. Unfortunately, the Boss is not among them.

The Shark

He's as elusive as James Bond, as hypnotically persuasive as Elmer Gantry. He's smooth, well-dressed, knows his way around. On his arm, you feel like part of the perfect couple, and when he speaks, he may choose his words from among the two or three languages he's fluent in for effect. He may be a movie star or a telephone lineman, but if he's a Shark, his hair is perfectly clipped, his underwear imported.

In action, the Shark will charm you, awe you with his boundless energy and charismatic style, promise you anything. But don't be surprised if he forgets your phone number. He'll deceive you, construct elaborate lies, cause you enormous unhappiness and be completely confused and hurt when you leave him. He is constitutionally incapable of making a direct statement. Ask him a question and he becomes as slippery as salad oil. He'll sit on the fence, be suggestive or cryptic and hope you guess his needs correctly. At his most impossible, he talks in riddles, zapping you with mixed messages, contradicting himself as the conversation moves along. If you point out inconsistencies in his logic, he'll accuse you of not understanding him!

The Shark can be verbally cruel, with a quotable edge of hilarity. He likes to insult you and make you laugh at the same time to set you off balance. He can be insufferable, taking his frustrations out on you. While you're recovering from an onslaught, he expects you to tell him what a great guy he is. The Shark tends to seek reassurance from those he's just skewered.

Wily and exploitative, he lives to con you. He'll find out what you want and dangle the sweet bit before you. Do you want *him?* A job *through* him? To meet someone he *knows?* He'll put you through a trial by fire before doing something for you or striking a deal. It doesn't matter. What matters is that you're smitten, and he won't let you go. Tell him he's self-centered, a user and a liar and slam out the door. He'll call (even crawl) back, begging your forgiveness, his voice swelling with choked-back tears, his eyes moist and pleading. He may even propose marriage to you. Most likely, he'll want to collect you, like a trophy. When you've got something the Shark needs for his comfort or to get ahead—social prestige, genealogy, celebrity, enough money to pamper him, your complete devotion—then he's yours.

The Shark isn't usually a criminal, though tales of rascality get his blood pulsing a little harder. But he becomes intoxicated by neatly bending the rules without actually breaking them or being held accountable. When he breaks rules, his justification is not getting caught. He often excels at pulling off "white-collar" crimes. Materialistic, Sharks are impressed by the visibility that accompanies prosperity. They like walking into the trendiest doctor's office, restaurant, disco or beach resort in fifteen-hundred-dollar custom-made suits. Sharks don't like to agonize over choices—they want the top of the line only.

Their con artistry is consecrated to using others for their own gratification. People are simply a means to their ends, and if they can cheat you of your fair share while justifying the insult to you, they will. Suggest a heart-to-heart talk and you'll find that the Shark's self-disclosure is all hot air, like the other "intimate" conversations you've had with him. You can expect to hear what he thinks you want to hear.

Sharks are lusty and sexually aggressive and often demand frequent sex. Sex is not necessarily for pleasure with the Shark—it's more an act of conquest. If you remember the boy from your youth who argued, "If you love me, you'll go all the way," and left you when you didn't, you'll recognize him in the Shark, merely grown older. Marry him, and he'll demand sex as proof of your love, but don't expect much tenderness after the act. He draws back into himself and rolls over, frightened of being vulnerable and having you know it.

At one extreme, the Shark may be so involved in his life of scheming and high adventure, subterfuge and deal-juggling that he looks for expression and release in drug or alcohol abuse. This Shark is distrustful, edging toward paranoia at times, constructing false evidence of your disloyalty to him. He's a sad case, and a balanced marriage to him is nearly impossible. His relationships with women are often tumultuous and combative. Intimacy on his terms is characterized by excessive demands or insatiable sex or both. He suffers from serious depression, inability to hold a job and outbursts of violence.

The shark, the predatory fish upon whom he is patterned doesn't have a single bone in his body. Its skeleton is all cartilage—much softer stuff. The Shark in the fifteen-hundred-dollar suit will deny it with his last breath, but he's not Jaws. He's much softer stuff, too.

The Golden Boy

Though not quite up there with stratospherically tough guys like the Boss or the Shark, the Golden Boy wields his own style of power play, which can be just as psychologically fatal. Charming and boyish, he coaxes out your motherly feelings. Please love him unconditionally. If he can't arouse the mother in you, he'll accept your devoted twenty-four-hour room service. Please take care of him no matter what condition he's in. Like a soufflé, he must be served *now!* Golden Boy's a love junkie, and if you are inclined to supply the drug, *you're* hooked.

Golden Boy suffers from a paradoxical dilemma: He's afraid of being alone but tires easily of the company he keeps. He's *bored*. "*You're* boring" are his parting words to you after kicking over a lamp. That lamp was not among the household objects he paid for. He'll return for those things and *you* can pack them—including the steaks in the freezer and the spring-operated pants hanger he let you use for your skirts. Cost is not the motivating force in claiming his possessions. He's got a serious problem about giving to others, even incidentally. So if he's on his way out (and by the way, he'll mention, the break-up is your fault), he wants what's rightfully his, since he paid for it, including what's left of the groceries. Ask him where he's going if you want another demonstration of mounting rage. You already know. He's ensnared another woman (or returned to his mother) and you'll hear of her soon enough.

The core of the Golden Boy's personality has his own initials carved in it. He's a classic narcissist, a dreamer with self-aggrandizing fantasies you are expected to encourage. He smiles winsomely to get his way; he flatters you unmercifully, strokes your ego and tells you what you want to hear—until he has you in the palm of his hand. Remember the night you met, had a drink together? More accurately, *he* ordered a Coke, no ice, and explained, wincing just once, that he'd just recovered from a "bug," but *don't worry about it.* He smiled at you rapturously, moved in closer and enfolded you in a molten gaze that described you as the most fascinating woman he'd ever known. You were in love. He invited himself for dinner. Two months later, there was nothing you wouldn't do for him. And you told him so.

He already knew. By then he had "spilled his guts"— offering you riveting stories of lost family fortunes (just when he most needed the cash), turgid accounts of dead siblings and aunts with incestuous bents (his tortured adolescence), impassioned tales of ambitions thwarted by jealous rivals (his frustrated professional life) and how much he's going to love you. This is the bottom line.

Love controls him and he'll use it to control you. It's his drawing card. The pity is, he can't *be* loved enough and he can't give love at all. Approval is his preoccupation. He's not quite sure he's real unless others are reacting to him, reminding him how original, smart, handsome, hard-working or appreciated he is. Criticism is toxic to his spirit. He can't bear reproach, or civilized, well-intentioned suggestions for improvement or guidance. Expect a tantrum or pouting withdrawal. If you insist that he listen to your problems, he'll nod and make sympathetic noises as you talk. Notice his eyes; they're glazed over. He's somewhere on the moon. His capsule returns to earth when he's heard enough—three or four minutes' worth. Then he'll stroke your hair and say everything will be just great, so be nice and make him some eggs.

Don't try to figure out his convoluted logic. It all

has to do with manipulating you to get what he wants as soon as possible. Waiting is not one of his strengths. He's short-tempered and frustrated easily—he's not accustomed to non-instant gratification, a result of a very pampered boyhood. Golden Boys were the kids bailed out of tussles with the law or with peers by an overly protective and very adoring parent who will never admit that Golden Boy is flawed or wrong.

He likes being married, especially if the woman he chooses indulges his whims and babies him. He may actually find greater sexual adventure in marriage to a woman he can dominate, sometimes demanding submission at inappropriate times and places. He likes being "done to," while assuming a macho veneer. His jealous streaks surface in social situations and he's likely to accuse a wife of flirting with adulterous intent. He's terrified at the thought of your leaving him, but more afraid another man will steal you away. He's really inadequate at heart, a spoiled small boy who doesn't have the skills yet to make it in the world without a strong emotional back-up team, which unfortunately encourages his dependency, not his maturity.

The Shadow

He's many men—all of them lonely, angry, haunted by a bitter past, withdrawn and *so fragile* he uses insensitivity to others as an effective shield from any more emotional pain. This man has mastered neutrality. More than anything, he wants to be accepted, but his very lack of flavor or depth creates comment. However, he sees himself as wiser, stronger and more morally correct than any other man. He hopes others will respect him for what he *doesn't* say or *might* be thinking— but of course, *you* supply the lofty heroic thoughts and endow him with greater depth than he has.

When he's less heroic, he's a grumbling doomsayer who loves tales of family tragedy. In any conversation he'll contribute a negative slant on any topic from the weather to God. The Shadow can be philosophical at times, though he never quite agrees or disagrees with you. He responds in noncommittal phrases, secretly hoping you extract a meaning that *dis*pleases you from his vagaries. He likes to unnerve you. Don't push him to be too decisive. He much prefers to observe others and reveal few of his own feelings.

One reaction he doesn't hide is suspicion. He's simply and openly suspicious of strangers, new neighbors, foreign accents. He may worry about your European hairdresser. "Who is *he?* Where did he get the cash to buy his shop? How long has he been in this country?" Should they meet and your hairdresser asks him, "So, I hear you're in the used car business, how are things?" The Shadow will deliver a cryptic answer, or *no* answer. He resents being questioned at all—it infringes on his privacy. He's much better at staring others down than leaving the room.

In real life with you, he never clarifies his problems. He'll impart little information, expect you to guess his motives and feelings—and then be hurt when you guess wrong. Some Shadows don't even offer up tidbits for you to speculate about—they'll just deny, flat out, that anything's amiss. ("Wrong? What could be wrong? *Why do you ask?*")

The Shadow needs to validate his view of the world, wherein he's right and everyone's out to prove him wrong. Denial protects him. Of all his shortcomings, the one quality that most describes him is an inability to notice or analyze his own actions. He doesn't see what he's doing, hear what he's saying or feel what he's feeling. A Shadow will deny the cruel and negative comments he's flung at you seconds after you repeat them back to him.

Shadows suffer from terribly low self-esteem. Usually, he cannot give love and will deflect signs of love, when they come at him, like bumper cars at an amusement park. To him, accepting love is tantamount to a terrifying uphill climb on a sheet of ice. Love scares him, embarrasses him. He usually comes from a home where there was little demonstration of love, tenderness or sharing. The Shadow promised himself at an early age that he would never be hurt again.

Unlike the boss, Shadows don't have great charm or charisma. The Boss creates a following, but the Shadow follows the Boss and tries to emulate his style, capture some of the magic. The Shadow only sees the tough stuff, though, and a Shadow with an additional veneer of tough stuff is a man you should run from.

Shadows run from *you* at a high trot, but prefer to see it as your rejection of *them*. There's a side to the Shadow that's self-pitying and begrudging. Do you want sex? Do you need tenderness? They're not interested, and how *like* you, comes the accusation, to *not* notice *they're* not in the mood. Even if they are, they're not—they get an odd kind of pleasurable twinge from being contrary. Giving implies surrender, a position they find intolerable.

Like white bread, the Shadow has only the appearance of substance.

The Banker

The Shadow can assume a slightly healthier form, less hazy but still basically devoted to avoiding real intimacy. This Shadow, more appropriately called the Banker, lives by his own self-regulated restrictions. He's often a workaholic, getting greater satisfaction from things than from people. He has an investment in appearing likeable, and makes an effort to belong. The Banker can tell a joke, even if he can't take one.

His relationships are weighed and measured. His mother gave you his grandmother's ruby ring when you got engaged. He got nothing but a lasagna dinner. He calculates the situation quickly: His mother is slighting him—who are *you* to get a family ring! He cannot see that the gift is for both of you—a loving gesture from his mother, not an attempt to exclude him. He gets no pleasure from another's joy, even if he's indirectly involved.

The Banker has money, or at least he dreams about it a lot. He wishes he were "old money," with awesome assets to back up the good family name. New money captures his heart, too, from lottery millionaires to OPEC sheiks. Numbers impress him, and he tends to manage his own accounts with three guiding mottoes: "If you've got it, keep it," "I am what I have," and "What do *you* need it for?" Getting him to part with money is always a battle.

The Banker has limited ambitions; he's less driven and less self-confident than the controlling Boss. He's the "good enough" personality—whatever he's got is good enough. He'll have complaints about his good-enough purchases, never quite getting the connection between the price he's willing to pay and the quality of what he gets. He's less abrasive than the Shark, but he couldn't compete in a verbal parrying-to-the-death with one and hope to win. He's every corporation's reliable son, or the favorite son's persona non grata.

He also is the American mother's favorite son-in-law. If your marriage to the Banker ends in a devastating crash, your mother (along with your friends) might suspect *you* of causing the problems. Everyone's impulse is to take his side at first. How could this solid, reliable, traditional, upstanding, all-around nice guy be so bad? Did you forget to serve him dinner? To please him in bed? Did you burn his stock certificates? Dress like Tina Turner to assert your individuality on the night of the Banker's Ball? Did you assume marriage to him would be balanced neatly at fifty-fifty and upon telling him so, cry when he laughed?

Money turns him on—and the more he accumulates, the more he believes it proves he's somebody. He wants it all—he's not good at sharing. How can you accuse him of being cheap? He's putting it away for you. Call him a tightwad, a Scrooge, miserly, scabby, unchristian—what do you want? Isn't his weekly allowance enough for you? He needs control of his money, and your interest in it threatens him in two critical ways. He secretly fears it's just his cash you're fond of, not him, and that you may trick him into signing it all over to you. W. C. Fields was the classic parsimonious Banker in real life. He was said to have opened hundreds of bank accounts across the country under assumed names that only he knew. Fields was buried with those undisclosed names, and his heirs had no idea where to look. The Banker arguing with you over the price of pantyhose would be fond of Fields's approach to investments.

What drew you to the Shadow or Shadow Banker in the first place? The withdrawn Shadows are *safe*—they don't demand much in expression of feelings and often aren't very sexual after the initial rush early in marriage. You can be the star with a Shadow husband—he's happy to let you be the popular one, getting the invitations he could never attract on his own. He's not much of a risk taker, essentially very traditional, cautious, dependable, The Shadow will keep you out of trouble, balancing your optimism with a strong dose of reality. At his best, his silences are welcome, even calming.

The Loser

When the Shadow casts a dimmer, more attenuated version of himself, he's the Loser—the man who just can't get it together and won't face the reasons why. The Loser may actually be ambitious, and his conversation often focuses energetically on the higher plane he strives for. Unfortunately, he's more likely to commandeer the takeover of companies (or countries) while drifting off to sleep than to activate his plans during waking hours. He dreams of power, but feels powerless.

ship with you. He's stone soup—inappropriate, gray and completely lacking in flavor.

The Loser is insecure, so he'll require affirmation at patience-destroying intervals. This is a man who'll say, "Why don't we take a trip to Bermuda this Easter? That is, if we're still together by then/you haven't left me/you haven't left me for another man." The Loser waits for you to announce your departure, and may even hasten your decision by his torturous questioning. If you need to end the relationship to save yourself from him, you're literally inviting him to a suicide *attempt*. He may steer his car into a tree at ten miles an hour, incurring a bump on his temple, or hit himself on the head with a heavy alarm clock. Dizzyish and bleeding from a minor scalp wound, he'll stumble to your doorstep to collapse.

The Loser has his boyish charm. That's what drew you to him. But he's a boy in need of missionary work—and you'll be his Mother Teresa until you tire of saving him from his own inadequacies. He'll adore your help, even worship you for your ability to get ahead in this world. Both of you will eventually know he's not up to achieving, no matter how much clout you have in getting him a job or keeping him out of trouble. And trouble tempts a different type of Loser.

The Blaster

The thin-skinned Loser with his quizzical look and palms out asking for emotional alms has an alter ego in the Blaster—a thicker-skinned Loser with fists of fury. The Blaster has a temper. His first memory may have been of paint-chipped walls or of nursery walls papered with blue-chip stock certificates, but either way he's society's victim and he's fighting mad. He looks for your sympathy with prolonged tales of his wretched past, his thwarted opportunities and how others have blocked his path to success.

The Blaster is sometimes a physically violent person, duplicating his own abused childhood by being abusive to his family. He's the bully who starts a fight because you or anyone else looked at him "funny." Infantile impatience marks his style. He's petulant and will kick over the table if he loses a game of checkers. He'll pull the phone out of the wall if he wants your attention, that second. The Blaster who is less physically threatening uses verbal terrorization, which is just as wounding and still draws blood. He likes to create situations rife with discord and dissatisfaction and build visions of a gray and dusty future. He'll attack you when you're most vulnerable. He'll laugh and be unsympathetic if you get an obscene phone call that frightens you. Defend yourself from his crippling words and he's happy— he gets to fight!

Blasters believe they can't rely on anyone but themselves. They set up traps for you and others to make themselves right. In business, they'll use stalling techniques, withhold necessary information, reschedule meetings, then cancel, then reschedule. They change the rules if they get the chance, and reject what they okayed the day before. They'll demand to see what you've done and when it's inadequate—which it will be—they spit out criticism through clenched jaws and tell you how put upon they are. They like humiliating you and will be happy to fling your work across the room, if it's light enough and it's at all aerodynamically possible.

When you know a Blaster you'll understand how they accuse you of the precise inadequacies they've shown—inability to be direct, to make a decision, to share information, to plan together, to talk things out grownup to grownup or to be efficient.

At home, the nontrusting Blaster will accuse a wife of infidelity (especially if she's looking good one night at dinner), lack of interest, poor financial management, whatever. It's usually a giveaway—the Blaster's probably either having an affair, contemplating one or a poor money manager himself. He's a stone sandwich—inappropriate, hard and impossible to savor.

Why We Must Break the Mold

You've met the seven types of Junk Food Heroes most likely to be associated with problems in love relationships. And you might have caught sight of a lover, spouse or parent in the Banker or Shark; a brother in the Golden Boy, a little of yourself in the Boss, a few of your fears in the Loser, someone you fear in the Blaster. This is important.

We must recognize patterns of attraction and behavior that repeatedly hurt us. These men are capable of altering our behavior, restricting our emotional lives, living for their own best interest while exploiting us. Junk Food Heroes who have invested effort in never making us feel good will be sure to get *their* way. Those of us who have invested time in feeling good by making *them* better people will never get *our* way!

Unhealthy personalities gravitate toward other unhealthy personalities and form unbalanced relationships. This is a fact of life. The chance of finding fulfillment in love decreases the more we pursue mutually destructive ends. The relationship may be one of chemistry and fire—but it's all pyrotechnics, and the payoff is pain.

Is there an ideal love that works? What is it like?

To begin with, it is a peer relationship between people who see each other as equals.

What we're reaching for is altruistic egoism, which simply means: As I do for myself, I do for you; as I do for you, so will I do for myself. With enlightened self-investment we can recognize that there really is a payoff for everything, but that one partner's winning does not mean the other partner loses. There's trust—and one can say to the other, "I believe that you are faithful and committed because you're like me and I'm like you." With altruistic egosim, love doesn't demand submission to a controller, game-playing with an exploiter, excessive attention to a fearful, fragile ego. One person is not consuming the other. Altruistic egoism feels good and tastes good and doesn't leave a bitter aftertaste. The participants are two people who know how to give and receive love, who find it easy to reveal themselves and do so judiciously. They're capable of building an intimate relationship as happy, competent, responsible partners.

In a balanced relationship, one in which each partner seeks what is good for the other, as well as what is good for him- or herself, you can, to some degree, be dependent on another person for a feeling of heightened esteem. And that's okay. It means you want that person, and on occasion *need* him—but not so exclusively that if something bad happens to him, your life will start its final chapter. A balanced relationship makes it possible to cherish memories and not focus on loss, to love and enjoy the other person as he is, not just for any externals he may bring to the relationship. A balanced relationship allows goal-setting, not only on individual terms, but also as a couple, a unit. The couple decides what's right and what needs repair. Goal-setting helps couples measure the progress of their relationship over the course of time, and being mature and concerned, they give themselves the time to meet the goals they choose.

Junk Food Heroes need praise, adoration, an audience, and they want *you*. They cannot live without you, though they'll go to great lengths to deny it. For them to survive, they need a *reaction* from you—without a victim, a bully is just a frightened man, not a menace. You'll react if the man is tuned in to your needs, but the good news is that you *can* tune him out, defuse his power when he's just warming up. A patient told me about a party at which a Shark, her bête noir, slunk toward her. As he opened his mouth to say something, she put in quickly, "Hello, this won't work, goodbye!" and walked off. "I know it was rude," she explained, "but I had to save my life. I looked at him and knew I'd be doomed. It was better than saying, 'Hello, I'm sorry, I can't resist you.' "

Listen to your instincts and listen to what the man's saying—early on in the relationship. Watch his behavior. Then keep these following guidelines in mind.

How to Spot a Junk Food Hero

• He says one thing and does another. If you point it out, he'll promise to change, but repeat the quirk again.

• He insists he's right, even if he's glaringly wrong. He cannot take the slightest criticism or any nonglorifying observation of his personality.

• He makes you feel that he's never quite there—that he's slipping out of your arms.

• He says, "It's my way or the highway." He calls all the shots.

• He wants you to be around when he wants you to be around. You have no say in the dating arrangement.

• Everything he earns is his and he exacts *blood* for any small gift or for any favor he does for you.

• He keeps you on your toes by demonstrating an interest in other women. He likes to make you feel challenged or inadequate, or both.

• He watches you for any signs of individual growth or interest in any activity that doesn't include him.

• He needs you to flatter him, but he won't return the favor.

• He answers questions that are directed at you, telling others what you think, how you feel and what you're doing.

Resisting the Temptation of Junk Food Love

Not everything you want is good for you—you should be able to turn down a hot fudge sundae when you're on a diet, or even when you *aren't* on a diet. If you must have a taste, come to terms with taking that one spoonful and knowing it's a snack—not the main course. If you can push away the rest of the dish, get up from the table and feel a renewed sense of self-esteem, your life will change. One thing is certain— just as hot fudge is incapable of transforming itself into pasta primavera, so is a Junk Food Hero unwilling to change for you.

If you go into a relationship knowing what makes you comfortable and happy and what creates chaos and pain, you are halfway toward getting what you want. When you tell a man who you are and he says and does the very things that make you unhappy, then both of you know he has chosen to relate to you like a Junk Food lover. You cannot change him, and you must now make *your* choice. Can you *live with* his idiosyncratic behavior, as he uses your weaknesses against you, or do you *leave?* These are the only two choices open to you. Junk Food lovers don't change unless they have something to gain. You can spend a lifetime plotting ways to build his character, getting him into therapy, tricking him into treating you well, but why do it if you are left drained, miserable, unfulfilled and not cared for in ways that tell you you are cared for?

This is the difference between packaging and content. If a man's basic values and lifestyle, integrity and good will all serve to show love for you, what does it matter how he dresses or where he works? Once you opt for the sweet guys, you will have a greater chance for positive interactions. If you exist as equals—if neither of you wants to demean the other—you'll have a giving partner who'll love you with generosity and kindness.

One taste of that generosity and you'll be able to resist Junk Food Heroes forever.

Positive interaction is a basic human need, which is why so many people persevere in their search for love or marry so many times. Positive interaction is the key to a harmonious relationship and it must be developed and maintained *day by day* in word and deed: *You're important to me . . . I enjoy you . . . It's nice to have you home . . . I love you.* These are words the Boss, the Shark, the Loser, the Shadow, the Blaster, the Golden Boy and other Junk Food Heroes may begrudge you. Strong personalities like to *limit* your positive interactions, yet keep you tantalized and dissatisfied. They're the men you *serve,* not the men you *deserve.*

Junk Food Heroes Are Hazardous to Your Health

What brings you back to them is your fatal flaw, that part of your personality that says, "This is all I deserve and I'm lucky to have it." This belief system draws you to the men least likely to make you happy. What fantasies about love do you perpetuate that make you hungry for love? What's your *fatal flaw?* Let's find out.

3

Hungry for Love

"I HAVE a dream," Toby, a thirty-eight-year-old woman, confides in me. "I'm sitting in my favorite restaurant with six wonderful men. The lights are dim, kind of amber. I'm dressed in black. All eyes are on me. I raise my glass and tip it to each man. They're anxiously waiting for me to speak. Finally, I say with a sweet smile, 'And the fifth runner up for my hand in marriage is . . .'"

Dorothy, a trial lawyer in her mid-fifties, is speaking to me about the man she's been married to for thirty years. "I'm waiting to love my husband, I mean *really* love him. I want that rush, that feeling of urgency when he walks into a room. I've been loyal to him, but I don't think I love him," she explains. "In all this time, I've never told him I feel something for him. I never knew what to say."

Evelyn's husband calls her "bulldog," even in the presence of others, no matter how Evelyn pleads with him to stop. He says he can't help it because of her pale skin, square face and, he reminds her, because she's "getting a little jowly" as she moves into her late thirties. "Larry rarely speaks to me face to face," Evelyn confesses. "He talks to me over his shoulder, from behind a newspaper or looking at his dinner plate. He plays the macho game and no matter how I try to please him, it's never enough. I know my marriage isn't working, but I can't seem to leave. At least with Larry I have a place as *someone's* wife."

Though each of these women seeks love differently, they have one thing in common when it comes to love: They're ruled by a fatal flaw.

Take Toby. The scope of her romantic fantasy makes us laugh, not at her, but in recognition of our own picturesque imaginings. We've "been there" too. Toby's award ceremony sets her up as the coveted prize for six breathless men. In her dreams she's surrounded by suitors she conquers six at a time. She wants love from every man—but paradoxically, six men aren't enough and one is too much. Her fatal flaw is that she must be the star, attract every man, compete with every woman and always win the winner. In real life, she chooses men who conquer *her*. They're overbearing, controlling and capricious; she's suppliant, adoring and ultimately dominated.

Dorothy longs for the unattainable lover who would leave her breathless and, even in her fifties, clings to this image as if it were a reasonable dream. In her mind, Dorothy perpetuates a romantic ideal that is so specific her husband could never fulfill it. Her fatal flaw is a demand for perfection. Love must be perfect. "My lover must have every quality I desire. He must fulfill me exactly as I wish every day. He cannot have flaws or fail in anything. Since this is impossible, of course, I can never be satisfied." For over thirty years of marriage, her husband's been denied the pleasure of hearing that she cares about him, and she has denied herself that pleasure too. He hasn't been everything to her, so she makes him feel like nothing. Dorothy might have the happy ending she craves if only she could say "I care" to her own husband!

And then there's the case of Evelyn and Larry—a classic example of the lovesick wife and the cold-sick husband. Evelyn was desperate for love and selected someone who had little of it to give. Larry starves his wife for affection and attention. A sensitive woman, she married a man to complement her, to fill all the empty places. He's a man who's amused by Evelyn's sensitivity. He calls her "bulldog" to toughen her up, he says.

Evelyn's fatal flaw is wanting to be rescued from herself and life. She looked for someone who was everything that she was not, but as so frequently happens, she overcompensated and selected someone at the other extreme. Larry is as terrified of life as she is, but his stong coating of "macho" hides his feelings of inadequacy.

Many of us can identify with Evelyn's situation. Like her, we needed the security of marriage but did not feel safely married with the man we chose. Evelyn stubbornly holds on to a marriage that can destroy her chances for happiness forever. It's easier to stay in a relationship and be treated shabbily than to leave and have to trust yourself. Even if that permits a life of dignity, it's still a life alone! And though Evelyn may not see it, she romanticizes her lot with Larry. She acts the put-upon wife, and others grant her sympathy and offer suggestions for keeping Larry from taking her for granted. For her, love is an issue of control, wherein she's powerless. She believes, ultimately, that finding yourself in love means you actually *lose* yourself.

Our Fatal Flaws

Toby, Dorothy and Evelyn each have a fatal flaw that dooms them to make the same mistakes in love over and over again, or to remain in the same unhappy situation without making changes for the better. What exactly are these flaws and where do they come from? They evolve from many emotionally loaded experiences early in life. Think of a fatal flaw as a weakness that is triggered under certain circumstances—the kind that tend to stop us cold, get us into the same predicaments time after time. *I couldn't help it. I don't know what came over me. I thought it would be okay this time!* We can hear ourselves make excuses like these almost fatalistically.

That's the key to why we find it hard to let go of our fatal flaws. We believe they're as much a part of us as the color of our eyes—unchangeable. Because they germinate when we're young, they seem to be natural parts of our personality, and we give them power. And fatal flaws *do* have power. They have the knack of preserving history and surfacing at any time to help us relive it. Fatal flaws favor tempestuous relationships in which doubt, illusion and extremes of behavior control reason and block chances for equanimity. Fatal flaws, more than anything, show us how we are hungry for love. And it's a hunger that feeds on itself.

Toby, Dorothy and Evelyn hold on to self-defeating fatal flaws because of this hunger. My guess is that they started out with good intentions: "I only wanted . . ." What happens, though, is that they didn't get what they wanted because the fatal flaw took over. Here's how each woman describes her flaw, and what it really means.

Toby: "I want to be wanted by the most desirable man, and I always give him my life in return. He just winds up taking it and leaving me with nothing but pain."

Toby's real fatal flaw: Toby's propensity for Bosses, exploiters and narcissists exacts a stiff price. Actually, Toby may need the extreme behavior of the conqueror in order to feel more confident of her own femaleness. If the man is also driven to achieve, so much the better. She thinks she is known by the company she keeps, and if the man who desires her is himself socially desirable, she feels a greater sense of importance, of belonging.

Her real fatal flaw, then, is a lack of self-esteem. Filtered through her own particular romantic imagery, her fragile ego demands power and status to affirm her. Toby believes she's as good as the men who want her.

Dorothy: "In a moment of weakness, I married the first man who said he loved me. He's a nice guy, but I will go to my grave never knowing real love because of him."

Dorothy's real fatal flaw: Dorothy considers herself a logical person—she's a lawyer and her mind is trained in logic. But to protect herself, Dorothy has applied a convoluted illogic to her emotional life and calls it fact. She predicts the outcome of her love relationships by the well-tested "self-fulfilling-prophecy" method, which is one way to make sure you don't get what you want. And *that* could be exactly what she wants. Dorothy doesn't want to stay in a passionless marriage, but she won't allow her own feelings for her husband to emerge and risk reciprocity. Nor will she abandon the marriage to seek the heart-stopping love that she imagines is eluding her.

Dorothy's real fatal flaw is also a lack of self-esteem. She's really thinking, "I can't bear to admit that I may be a woman who doesn't arouse passion, and I can't face the fact that I might not be able to handle the passion if it came to me. It's better to be married to this nice, passive guy and not have to worry about it at all." Dorothy's fatal flaw is filtered through a rigid framework of biases about what constitutes love. To her, any other behavior that demonstrates caring—as with her husband—barely counts.

Evelyn: "I just want to be a good wife. I don't ask for much, but I get pushed around and humiliated instead."

Evelyn's real fatal flaw: Evelyn's fatal flaw is that she doesn't feel that she deserves more than she is getting. She's thankful to have a man. On most days the fact that he stays is enough. To have him leave would end her life; it would prove that what she fears is really true—she is unworthy of love. Whatever he gives her is better than what she can give herself. Besides, he recognizes her lack of worth and he stays anyhow. Who else would do that?

More Fatal Flaws

What's so fascinating about fatal flaws is their infinite variety and how they are expressed. You might, for example, become a psychological nun and give up looking for love. Or you might become attached to an unrealistic image of man—he must look, think and act in a certain way. As a result, you can't find anyone out there who fits the model. Maybe you seek comfort from life's pressures with food. You victimize yourself with excessive calories, taken in as "love." Like the psychological nun, you fear that no one could love you and take a hard line against relationships. ("Chocolate never says no.") A more contemporary example is the overachiever—that spectacular model of womanhood, the superwoman. She lives to compete with other women in every way. Winning proves she's the best. ("It's not enough that I'm in this world, I must *have* the world.") Then there are the women with obsessive personalities whose fatal flaws are grounded in anger and distrust. They examine every gesture and word, review every statement and re-experience every encounter over and over again looking for possible slights. Their fears of loss are so great that any innocuous gesture or remark can trigger unreasonable responses. ("If I don't protect me from the vultures out there, who will?")

Most of us can look at our lives and, after a moment of deliberation, point to an overwhelming flaw. Do any of these sound familiar?

Fatal Flaw: The Need for Love; or, I'll Do Anything So You Won't Leave Me. I Don't Want To Be Alone.

When Debbie became Hank's legal secretary it was a dream come true. Working for the most eligible bachelor in town fueled her dream of finding Prince Charming. She couldn't wait to show him how much he needed her. She began by running his errands—to the dry cleaner, a gift for his Mom, last-minute grocery shopping. It meant canceling her own appointments, but she felt it was a necessary beginning to forming an attachment. Soon she found herself overseeing his household, even preparing little dinners that he'd share with someone else. "You're the really important one," he told her. "I'm just not ready to make a commitment." Debbie's dates with Hank were last-minute affairs, which meant she broke other appointments to be with him. The final straw came when he had her make travel arrangements for two, obviously planning to take someone else while giving her instructions for house-sitting. That drove her into my office, but it didn't drive him from her fantasies. "I know when he comes back I'll see him again if he asks me. I want him in my life. He makes me feel special."

Fatal Flaw: The Need to Compete; or No One's Going to Give You Anything. If You Have to Step on Someone to Get It, So What?

When Jackie was around other women, she made them invisible. It's not that they literally disappeared, but that Jackie forgot they existed when men appeared on the scene. "Why are my friends so angry with me?" she complained. "Can I help it if men are immediately attracted to me? My friends are just jealous." But that wasn't really all there was to it. Jackie felt that her best chance of getting the right man was to get all men, and try she did. When one of her friends began dating a man Jackie liked, loyalty to a pal didn't stop Jackie at all. In fact, it made the game a little more interesting. "It's a jungle out there," she told me. "A girl has got to take care of herself. After all, aren't we all in competition for a man? Who are my friends kidding? They would do the same thing to me. We all jump in, go for the guy and let the best woman win. I just do everything I can to be the best woman. My friends are ticked because I get more attention than they do." Unfortunately for Jackie, her greedy fatal flaw shows up in her relationships with men as well as women. Behind the mask of just wanting to take care of herself and getting her fair share, she knows that she's really very lonely. Not only do her friends recognize her basic insecurity, but the men whom she fights so hard to get recognize it too, and often exploit it.

Fatal Flaw: The Need for Unconditional Approval; or, Criticism Means You Don't Like Me. I'm Terribly Sensitive and No One Understands Me.

Linda could never see that when social situations went wrong, she was partly to blame. Once, having dinner with her boyfriend's parents, she made a negative remark about women who didn't work outside the home. Later, her boyfriend suggested that this was a very tender area for his mother. His dad had been pushing her to take a job and she was really frightened about going out into the working world at her age. Linda's response was to totally overreact. "Don't make your mother's problems mine. I just made a little re-mark and if she's sensitive about that, that's her prob-lem. Don't take it out on me and make me feel like I'm some kind of a bad person because I made a perfectly innocent statement. I was just making con-versation and now you're picking on me the way you always do!" This type of response isn't unusual for Linda. At work, if her boss criticizes her reports or suggests that she's coming in to the office a little later each day, her response is typically dramatic. "You just don't appreciate me," is one of her favorite lines. Or, "No one knows how hard I work," or, "I have feelings, too. Why does everyone step on them?" In truth, Linda is a fairly critical person, always comparing herself to others and always feeling a little pale by comparison. In order to compensate, she feels, whatever she does must be perfect. For Linda, everything that she does must receive complete approval—her clothes, her con-versation and her work must be accepted without question or she begins to question the relationship. Even the most minor suggestion is taken as unfair criti-cism.

Fatal Flaw: The Need for Status; or I Can't Do It Myself, So I Must Have a Man Achieve It for Me.

When Marilyn met Micky she thought that all her prayers had been answered. Micky was going to be a doctor, but when he entered medical school, he realized that medicine was not for him. In addition to hating the sight of blood, he felt his life would not be his own and he would be at the constant bidding of patients who had a splinter and felt they needed major surgery. When he told Marilyn that he had changed his mind and no longer wanted a medical career, she was furious. "But your father's a doctor and you promised you were going to be a doctor. You're so bright. So what if you don't like it. After all, how many people really like what they do?" she asked. "The least you can do is finish medical school and go on and practice for a few years. Then if you don't like it, maybe you can get into something else; a business of some kind. Think of the life that we'll have if you're a doctor," she implored. "The country clubs, the respect, how could you do this to me?" Like many women who believe the fairy tales of youth, Linda wanted her prince to make it happen for her, and when he didn't, she turned on him for not living up to the standards she had set for their life together. Unfortunately, this is a fairly common scenario. Like Linda, many women who conform to the traditional stereotype of the passive, retiring female exert constant pressure on their husbands to achieve in their place.

Fatal Flaw: The Failure to Take Responsibility for Your Life; or, Some People Are Just Born Lucky. Everything Is Given to Them. Why Should I Even Bother to Change—Either You've Got It or You Don't.

When Susan came to see me, she never took off her coat and bundled herself into the corner of the couch. Sometimes she spent therapy sessions barely saying a word, just looking at me imploringly. "How can I help you?" I would say to her. "I don't know if I can be helped," she'd reply. But she was there and that was a beginning. "I'm married to a man whom I don't love. His mother lives with us and berates me daily. My children see me as a maid in my own home and I feel lucky to be alive at the end of the day. I guess it's the draw of the cards. I don't even know why I'm here," she said. "There's nothing that can change. This is just my lot in life."

But change she did. It didn't happen overnight, but fortunately for Susan, she was able to change her attitude. She was transformed from a woman who believed in the newspaper ads that tell you you can lose twenty-five pounds overnight while you sleep into someone who discovered that if she worked at something and showed discipline and spunk, she could reach her goals. Susan was forty when she came to see me and she was sure that her history would be her future. But she listened carefully when I told her that the only thing that was guaranteed in life was that the years would pass, that the one choice she really had to make was whether to fill them with something new and exciting or to just allow them to run their course without a steady hand at the helm. Today, Susan has a master's degree in psychology and works as a clinician in private practice. Hers is only one of many success stories that I could share with you. She was able to make the turn in her life by looking at herself in the mirror. Recognizing that her own behavior patterns were getting her into trouble, she was able to make some major changes after a few minor adjustments.

Almost all of these fatal flaws have a common source— our devalued sense of self-worth. There's a real link between a lack of self-esteem and various styles of loving or not loving. That link is the fatal flaw. Let's take a closer look at a few more that get women into trouble.

A Few More Fatal Flaws

False Pride: How Could He Do That to Me? I'll Show Him!

Clare, a new patient, wants to gain the strength to leave her husband and the reason she gives is adultery. Bob is having an affair with a younger woman in her apartment complex. It's been going on for five years and Clare has just found out about this indiscretion through a gossiping neighbor of "the other woman."

Clare is filled with rage. Does she feel betrayed? In her heart she knows it was a marriage of convenience. When she's questioned, Clare admits that the idea of betrayal is not the source of her anger or the reason she wants to leave the marriage. What is it? *Humiliation.* Clare says the word as if it were a deadly virus of an unspeakable nature. Her husband must be punished for humiliating her.

What disturbs Clare is not that she's sharing her husband, or even that her lifestyle is threatened, but that "everyone knew but me." For her, this is grounds for divorce. Is it?

The story of Clare's marriage unfolds from there. Married for twenty years, she and her husband have not gotten along for the last five—since he found someone else. There's been little emotional intimacy since then and when I ask if they have a satisfactory sexual relationship, Clare answers, "On occasion." On occasion is further explained as "very intermittently." Then very intermittently is clarified—once a year!

Bob hasn't asked for a divorce yet, and even if he's getting some needs met with his lover, he may not want out of the marriage. Whether his motive is inertia, economy, emotional commitment (unexpressed though it may be) or fear, he's still with Clare.

"I want a divorce. He can't do this to me," Clare snaps. I suggest that she look at some facts and have some foresight. What will happen if she gets a divorce? First, her husband is a sharp businessman and he will take most of their assets. He probably already has his accountants considering the possibility of their divorce. In the end, this couple would have planned to leave their money to their three children. But battling divorce lawyers, his and hers, will get a *huge* chunk of money and essentially become partners in this twenty-year marriage. Finally, I tell her that if she cared enough to marry Bob and live with him for two decades, why not put false pride out of her mind and see if it's possible to retrieve the marriage?

Knowing about Bob's affair is painful to Clare, but it has forced her to face long-denied evidence that the marriage is on the edge. Bob has been careful to shield Clare from his infidelity and Clare insulates herself behind the institution of marriage—at least she has that and can fool herself and others. But in the end, her pride is too hurt and she loses control. She wants to strike out. What should she do?

If she follows her impulse, she'll have her pride and the divorce she may not want once it's legal. False pride lives for appearances, preserving an image for others while sacrificing what one most wants. Is it worth the trouble to "look good" for people one doesn't even care about? If Clare wants her marriage, she'll have to go to Bob's office, walk in and say, "Today is the beginning of a brand new relationship for you and me. I don't want this marriage to end! I want you in my life. I'm willing to make some changes to make that possible. Let's not throw away our marriage without exploring the possibilities. You can always leave—but what will make you choose to stay? Let's meet and talk."

Clare has a choice: She can please others who she thinks will have greater respect for her if she divorces, or she can have a chance for real self-respect by honestly expressing her feelings, as vulnerable as she is. Bob will not turn her down. He's still committed, in his way, to the marriage. He will listen. If her attempt doesn't work, then she will know this: Giving a relationship your best shot is something you *can* be proud of. If it fails, she will always know she did her best.

If false pride prevails, this relationship will slip away

and Clare won't recognize how it really happened. In spite of her fatal flaw she must go forward. Its power will be lessened the moment she and Bob institute a plan to rebuild the marriage, or at least work out a separation agreement that will not devastate both of them—and will allow the possibility of reconciliation.

She has a choice: living with her fatal flaw and the losses it incurs, or giving herself a chance to face her vulnerability and recognize that rejection isn't terminal. It can give one an opportunity for growth, and the pain is a demonstration that one is alive.

Fear of Loneliness: I Can't Be Alone. Being with Anybody Is Better than Being Alone with Myself.

Nora is in a marriage characterized by inertia, and neither she nor her husband, Ted, can charge it with energy. Ted is an interesting man—he's my patient and has been for one year. Just recently, I discovered that Ted has been seeing another therapist through the entire time and never mentioned this to me. Nor has he told the other therapist, whom he's been seeing twice a week for three years, about me. Nora informed me of Ted's "secret" in a meeting I had with her. Ted can't make a commitment to his marriage or to his therapy.

Nora told me that Ted bores her and her marriage

is an empty one. Ted shows little interest in her and has no attachment to their one son, but he comes alive when he's off skiing or playing ball with his buddies. Nora stays with him because she feels comfort just knowing that he will be coming home at the end of the day. But in her heart, Nora wishes the man walking through the door were anyone but Ted.

Such thoughts upset her, and so to quell her anxiety, Nora goes shopping. What she buys puts her in debt, or more accurately, in debt to Ted. She stays with him because he is her only hook to survival—she cannot support her habits on her own. Her fatal flaw keeps her exactly where she is. To her, risking change is more terrible than mounting bills from irresponsible spending or being alone. Debt insures a bond.

Ted complains, but secretly he's pleased about Nora's fatal flaw. When Nora spends, he's assured that the marriage is not over by *her* choice. He's in tune with her weakness. She won't spend and leave him, because her spending binds her to him. How can she walk out when he's paying these bills? In Ted's mind, he's the great provider. So he too must stay. Nora makes sure Ted stays by never permitting the bills to be paid off. Shopping centers are very accessible, open every day, and Ted hasn't demanded she cut up her charge plates.

Nora is guilty about her extravagance, but it doesn't

stop her from getting into the car with an object in mind—buying something she doesn't really need. Spending also insures that she's never going to get ahead or get out of a dreary marriage where money, outgoing, is *the* source of togetherness.

I believe strongly that we arrange our lives in ways that protect our inadequacies, and we organize them so that we don't move forward. We're frightened, and often we're not able to identify what it is that frightens us. Nora and Ted are actually perfect for each other— they really are. They are both traditional people with little sense of adventure about life, tentative people who need to keep things as they are.

Many women stay in marriages because they either cannot take care of their own needs or believe they can't. Like Nora, they live in fear of ever having to take care of themselves, or be by themselves. Their fatal flaw is a willingness to trade their lives to a man who'll take care of them and be with them, which is more than they can do by themselves.

Nora has made a conscious choice to take on a dependent role and Ted agrees with it. If Nora ever wants to end this marriage she must take responsibility for the burden of debt by paying it off. As long as Nora indulges her fatal flaw, she'll remain unhappily dependent, unsatisfied with Ted, and digging a bigger hole for her marriage and herself to be buried in.

Self-Sacrifice: Please Let Me Please You so I Have a Purpose in Life.

The "Pleaser" believes that others come first and she comes second. She always listens to other people's opinions before offering her ideas. She won't wear white after Labor Day or leather boots after the first day of spring. In tune with the demands and standards of others, she cannot endure being wrong or suffering disapproval. She eagerly looks to others to lead; following gives her a sense of belonging, of purpose.

The Pleaser thinks it's her duty to help you get a job or a husband, be your therapist, mother, doctor. She'll take on chores she cannot really accomplish, just to get you on her side. She'll help a spouse or child through school by working at three jobs if she must. She's a friend to the world, and if her morals and self-esteem are in a particularly low phase, she'll do even more. She's the girl who can't say no.

The Pleaser is desperate to belong and be approved of and if she must deny her needs, she will. She doesn't want to bother anyone. She won't spend money on anything good for herself, exercising an extreme measure of self-sacrifice—martyrdom suits her.

Loretta embodies the Pleaser. A thirty-two-year-old woman on her own, Loretta has been working at a television station for five years. At work she is liked, but grossly underpaid. She struggles to get by, but doesn't know how to ask for more. She manages by being the company "good sport." Loretta is a slave, exploited. She's ever dependable, arriving earlier than anyone else, always ready to jump into her car and run an errand. She takes on extra assignments and she doesn't ask for payment. Loretta is thrilled to be working at the station, to be part of a powerful, glamorous entertainment empire.

Why can't Loretta ask for a raise and a promotion from her secretarial position? Because she needs her family of anchormen, visiting celebrities, production people, cameramen, talent coordinators and other staff members. The show she's assigned to operates on teamwork, and the team is the family that keeps Loretta alive, though her salary nearly starves her, literally.

Loretta came from a family in which she was never good enough. She grew up trying to meet impossible standards handed down from a competitive mother and a religious father. Criticism accompanied her to bed at night. If she brought home a report card with an average of 97, her parents coolly chastised her by asking, "Where are the other three points?" Loretta never stood up straight enough or was virtuous enough; if she was cheerful, her parents thought she was silly; if she was moody, they wondered why she had no sense of humor about herself. Her parents believed they were being critical for her own good, helping her to learn the lessons of life. Loretta was just "too sensitive," and they didn't want to "baby" her. All Loretta really wanted was a bit of warmth and acknowledgment of her achievements.

She found what she wanted at the television station. Here Loretta could do and give. The station loved her generosity, her willingness to be part of a great team working for a greater cause—the show. She loved it when they took from her, invited her to parties, included her in the day-to-day events.

Her television family may exploit her, but at least it's exploitation with a smile, a hug—and the home phone numbers of everyone at the station. Loretta feels connected to them all, and if she's used, at least they get pleasure from using her. Her parents were never pleased by what she did for them at home.

Goodness, sharing and generosity are part of Loretta's basic makeup—it's actually easy for her to share. But her fatal flaw takes these traits to the extreme. Such generosity is not in her best interest. She accepts the exploitation at the station because she finally feels wanted.

Loretta knows, deep down, that she's cheating herself. But she's afraid to ask for more money or a better position. If she did they might fire her or, like her parents, remind her about those three missing points. Belonging, being loved and maintaining the illusion of love has taken precedence over being respected and treated fairly.

How Fatal Flaws Begin

Fatal flaws arise from a persistence of negative thoughts from childhood. These negative feelings about past events influence our thinking in the present, and often result in a poor self-image. This, in turn, produces what David D. Burns, M.D., in *Intimate Connections,* called "twisted thinking"—illogical and invalid conclusions we reach about people, feelings and events. Thus, fatal flaws produce failed relationships and unhappy loves.

Can we rid ourselves of negative thoughts? Burns notes that the twisted thinking we get into seems "totally valid and convincing when we feel bad." Fatal flaws insure the bad feelings because we view the world through a curtain of suffering. So what can we do? Says Burns: "By putting experience in proper perspective you could think about the problem in a more objective and compassionate manner instead of ruthlessly ripping [yourself] to shreds. This is the *essence* of self-esteem. Anyone can feel good when things go his way, but when the chips are down, you have your greatest opportunity to love and support yourself." A little later we'll look at ways to get out of the well of negative feelings about ourselves. First, let's look at how it all began.

What happened to us, that we can't manage to love and to support our own efforts? How do we sabotage ourselves in familiar and tormented ways? Where did it all begin? The answer can be found in the kind of parenting we had. Think of the answers to these questions in your own life:

• Did your parents teach you to be obedient, regardless of cost? To be an extension of them, not a free-thinking individual?

• What was the goal of parenting in your family— for you and your parents to experience a mutual love, or was it a contest of wills?

• Did you feel you had to fulfill something they couldn't?

• Were you the "Cinderella" of the family—used by the others and made to feel as if you were an outsider, a step-child?

• Did you have fun with your parents? Did they like physical contact, the pleasure of each other's company, joint efforts to make something or do something?

• Were you an ornament, an entertainment piece, an achiever—but not a whole person?

• What did your parents teach you about love?

If They Didn't Like Themselves—They Couldn't Like You

Those of us who perceive that our parents' marriage was unhappy and conflicted, replete with inconsistency and anger, have much to contend with. It may have been a union in which the parents were really sibling rivals, in which struggles for power, control and domination were part of the daily ritual. It may have been a marriage in which one parent demanded that the other remain a child, in which there was no respect, genuine tenderness or affection. It may have been a marriage between two armed camps living under détente, civilized and friendly only when "keeping up appearances."

If you were raised in such a conflict-ridden home, you are suffering from the consequences of that marriage. Parents who themselves have low self-esteem cannot raise healthy children. Our parents had problems with the societal values of their time, pressures from their parents, and were forced to try to live up to standards they couldn't possibly meet. Then *we* came along, and they duplicated the parental behavior they knew. This repetition of poor parenting practices by generation after generation of parents can emotionally bankrupt the children—us—who are asked to live in ways that are contrary to their best interests and true nature. When others demand that we live as they do and be who they are and it pains us to do so, we grow protective shells and protective patterns of relating to others to shield ourselves from oppression. These are our fatal flaws—coping mechanisms devised in childhood, now no longer effective but still in operation.

Our parents contributed to the formation of these flaws with daily, insidious reminders. They inflicted blows to our fragile egos through cruel humor, brutality, neglect or even simple sentences that are undermining: "You sure don't measure up to what I wanted a daughter to be, do you?" A parent can be an alarmist, suffocating a child with his or her own fears and overprotection: "The world is cruel, so beware, trust no one, not even your so-called friends. You don't have to go out swimming with them—you might get hurt. Stay home with me." Sheer neglect can be devastating, too: "I'm not paying for your shoes— didn't I just buy you a pair six months ago? You cost too much to keep—don't bother me with your problems! If your old shoes hurt your feet, get used to pain. That's what life's about."

Maybe your parents' verbalization of love rang false, and you, the child, knew it wasn't genuine or from the heart. If your parents complimented you in front of strangers ("Adele is so pretty, so perfect, such a blessing, so talented. Sing for us, honey"), then booted you out of the room when company left, you probably felt deep inside a sense of panic ("What have I done wrong now?"). The narcissistic needs of the parent prevailed and the praise didn't communicate genuine warmth or love for the child.

A child's self-esteem can be eroded through repeated humiliation, by beatings and sexual misuse; it can also be hurt by parents who rule the family by very definite, stringent rules or extreme religious discipline. These parents compensate for their lack of ability to give love by turning their children over to something else, something that they think is a substitute for genuine affection—a cause, a dogma, an ideology.

A parent may show open or subtle preference for another child—the favored brother, the adored sister—giving unjust reproaches, unfair punishments and duplicity to the least favored. Self-esteem will suffer when parents wage a campaign to break a child's will. If the child shows resistance and fights, the parents may double efforts to suppress the child's anger, courage, independent thinking, even self-defense.

All these examples of parenting have at their core an emphasis on frustrating the child rather than loving him or her. Here's an important point to note: When a child is genuinely loved and when there is warmth, the child *knows* it. A child's instincts are keen because a child has no sophisticated defenses. *The child knows.* And when the child knows he or she is loved, the child can tolerate a variety of crises and traumas and come through.

Children know when punishment is deserved. Sometimes they even ask for it. But they're also aware that the true response shouldn't be a mindless pat on the head, humiliation or an intent to injure them in some way. They want to feel free to protest and feel *safe* protesting. But parents create stifling environments and think it's unhealthy for children to have their say. When their protest is repressed, children withdraw, taking blame upon themselves, feeling doubly unworthy of love. *I can't even speak in my own interest, I must be no good because no one will listen to me.*

Can you see how these early patterns shape our fears and behaviors as adults? Isn't it obvious that we select as mates people who treat us in a similar way so that we can try to prove to ourselves that we are lovable, only to fail again?

How Our Parents Left Us Hungry for Love

Children who feel unloved are not imagining things. They feel unwanted, unimportant and unworthy of attention because their parents *do not express love*. When parents are indirect, harsh or vague, children are forced to *guess* what they feel—and what choice do they have but to choose "unloved" over "loved"? This fills the children with such sadness! They conclude that they're unlovable because they have been unloved. And so they feel anxiety and their defense systems evolve.

Once our defense is up, we repress the conflict but still feel the suffering. Defenses work by getting through, fighting back, blocking out painful memories or unacceptable thoughts, but unresolved conflicts do not fade away. They just get buried under mountains of coverups. This is basically how we developed our fatal flaws. We learned to cope with the conflict by constructing a defense to deal with it, one that set us up to repeat the very conflict we abhor. In our early years we were starved for affection, doubted our lovability and devised coping mechanisms to survive. The mechanisms don't work for us, but we know no other way to cope. We still yearn for love, we have difficulty finding it and we persist in being attracted to the very people who cannot give it to us! The Junk Food Heroes mirror in their behavior what we missed in childhood. Or perhaps they are contemporary incarnations of our parent in style, word or deed. Either way, it is love we hunger for and affection we crave. How we've missed it!

Without the natural give and take of affection early in life, we develop an excessive dependence on the approval of others. And we get into trouble because that need is indiscriminate—*everyone* must like us! The need for approval or affection becomes disproportionate to the significance of the person. That's why the word "hunger" is so appropriate—it's as basic a need, and in the same way can be satisfied with enough empty calories to temporarily fill us up.

Unfortunately, this hunger for affection makes us wildly sensitive to the slightest rejection. The experience is universal. Someone says, "I'm busy," and we're undone! A man doesn't call when he said he would and we keel over. Another man leads us on, playing cat and mouse, and the game pains us but we can't stop playing.

Martha is typical of women who are hungry for love. She came from a home with a frightened, demanding mother who told her daughter to be grateful for any scrap of attention she got from a man. At twenty-six, she married a man ten years older, someone she worshiped. He encouraged her unconditional love. Over the years, she realized that Alan wasn't bright enough to fulfill his ambitions, that she had built a pedestal to hold a peanut. Desperate and disappointed, she signals her rejection of who he is to Alan in a thousand little ways. This shocks him. He remembers the bliss of her unconditional love—he felt safe with her. He didn't have to prove anything—just be there! Martha's criticism is scorching to him—he flinches at the slightest observation hinting of inadequacy on his part. He withdraws from Martha, finding safety in retreat, and she concludes that Alan's withdrawal is the very proof of what most frightens her—that she's unloved and unlovable after all, and her mother was right. She'll have to do with the scraps.

Martha doesn't have any experience in simply stating her feelings: "I care," "I love you," "I want us to be happier together. Tell me what you need." Nor can she disclose to Alan that her feelings are bruised: "I'm hurt by your withdrawal. I feel bad about it. Tell me what's wrong." Worse, Martha finds it impossible to admit that she's contributing to keeping Alan at a distance. Alan and Martha spin around in a vicious circle—neither giving, each wanting the other to relent first and give most, neither willing to make the other feel accepted. Neither is mature enough to express the very basis of their needs—love.

Hooray For Us

We may suffer with flaws, but in reality we are astonishing and diverse creatures with enormous potential. We tolerate pain valiantly to deliver our children. We bear hardship and adapt to having less without feeling stripped of dignity. Women freely give generous devotion and nurturing to others in their lives, and show enormous courage through life's vicissitudes. And women *can* discover who they really are after a lifetime of low self-esteem and repression and become willing to explore the breadth of their ability and the world for the first time even when they are in their forties, fifties, sixties or older.

Women get themselves into trouble because they're not tuned in to their own values and they don't have goals. If we could think them out—"What do I value in myself? What do I value in others? What's keeping me down? Where do I want to be ten years from now? Who's on my side?"—we could steer clear of some difficulties. When we clarify who we are, we can eliminate the people who trespass our boundary lines. We won't want to keep them in our lives. But when we keep the wrong people in our lives, those who provide a minimum of love, we continue and contribute to our self-effacement.

We should squarely face our fatal flaws and get better. At some point, we should say, "I don't want to suffer anymore. I want to be free of the past and have the chance to make choices." Women in a constant state of anxiety who have an abiding neediness for love to prove they are worthwhile don't have freedom. They're in bondage to themselves.

Take Off Your Makeup

Someone asked me? Why do we hesitate to look at the "basic stuff" of who we are? Do we fear we'll be damned as wrong, stupid, inadequate? Why do we cover ourselves up? Simply, it's this: We worry about what we're going to find once the probing starts—that it will be even worse than we fear. Will we discover that we're mean, cruelly manipulative? That we're the angry ones, starting fights we've blamed on others? That we're envious, unfair, avaricious, that we want to be first and best and we deny and begrudge our closest friends? Will we see how very less than perfect we are and want to deny it instead of admitting, "Well, that's who I am. I'll have to live with it because I really don't want to change and I actually like that part of me." Or, "I have to come to terms with the fact that I *am* flawed and I'll probably always be flawed, but I'll try to temper it and be watchful." Or, "I shall stay, but the flaw will go."

It is most important to go within and meet the terrors and monsters inside yourself. Examine them closely and say, "I'm not going to lie to myself about this." Acceptance of our virtues and flaws will help us begin to build self-esteem.

Detoxifying the Fatal Flaw

When you get right down to it, maturity is the cure for our fatal flaws. Maturity is an old-fashioned word that means "getting it all together." And once you *do* get it together, maturity is a continuing process. You don't reach a selected point and then stop and stagnate. These essential qualities make up maturity and help to identify it:

• You can give up the patterns of behavior that worked for you as a child but are *now* self-destructive flaws, or fatal flaws. You can come up with rational ways to detach yourself from them.

• You're willing to select the best parts of yourself to enhance and know that growth here is also continuing.

• You have the freedom to fully express who you are.

• You have an awareness of your limitations.

When you're mature, you're calmly cautious about trusting people. You don't think people are out to get you or get what they can from you. With maturity, you understand that the actions and motives of others aren't typically straightforward, but are often determined by a combination of self-protectiveness, expediency, unresolved fears and ambivalence. If you're honest, you know that you, too, have the same characteristics. Mature people don't feel helpless when they get in touch with human frailties and failings. They can sustain genuine friendships and promote goodwill, and they have a basic sense of faith and confidence in people who have proven themselves loyal and caring.

You begin to develop maturity by strengthening self-esteem. It's self-esteem alone that will allow you to have positive interactions with others and help you lose your taste for junk food love. Poor self-esteem leads you back down the same worn paths toward haphazard choices in men who will satisfy a minimum of your needs.

Building self-esteem isn't an overnight miracle. Knowledge about why you behave as you do or insight into others' behavior is good, but it's not enough. You must actively work to begin to rebuild your good self-image by understanding the life experiences that you have already had. Then you can begin to reject the messages of the past that came from your parents and led to the negative self-talk that you've been involved in. You can monitor your own behavior and vocabulary, identify your fears and take small steps toward overcoming them. Let me tell you exactly how it can be done.

Who Am I?

Make three lists on separate sheets of paper. List those of your characteristics that you like on one sheet, those that you don't like on a second, and changes that, if made, would make you feel better about yourself on a third. Here are two examples:

Example One: Debby, a Thirty-Year-Old Housewife

- *Characteristics I Like*

Pretty
Slim
High energy
Love my children
- *Characteristics I Don't Like*

Resent my husband
Uneducated
Angry at mother sometimes
Jealous of working friends
- *What I'd Like to Change*

Get a part-time job
More education
Learn how to say no to my mother without guilt

Debby feels that if she could work on those three wishes, she would heighten her self-esteem. What she must do now is select one of the wishes, break it down into small steps, visualize the goal and make a commitment to having the discipline, assertiveness and inventiveness to meet the goal.

Example Two: Arlene, a Thirty-six-Year-Old Working Woman

- *Characteristics I Like*

Bright
Ambitious
High standards for men
- *Characteristics I Don't Like*

Lonely
Lonely
Lonely
- *What I'd Like to Change*

I wish I was in love
Get a raise
Have more friends

Like Debby, Arlene must answer some questions: "What can I do to bring about these changes? What is the worst thing that can happen if I take the risk of bringing about these changes? Is that worst possible scenario really so terrible? Whom do I have in my world to say nice, supportive things to me when I need them; to encourage me to meet my goals? Can I ask that person or those persons for the support that I need? What do I do to contribute to my loneliness?"

Here are some things you can do to help bring about your own changes.

Change Your Thinking and Your Desires

• Think about the goal that you want to reach and visualize reaching it—think of a happy ending. Rehearse in your own mind the steps that are necessary to arrive at your goal. If you need to enlist the support of others, don't assume that they will not be available to help you. Ask them.

• Separate yourself psychologically from the negative, unhappy people in your life who will never give you positive responses. Stop going to them for support. Don't presume that you will fail and label yourself a failure.

• Describe the behavior that gets you into difficulty and seek out small ways of changing it. Reach out to a circle of friends, beginning with just one person, for support. Don't isolate yourself or feel that you have to do it all alone.

If you feel these techniques cannot work for you because you need a supportive individual to help, then try the process below.

Building Self-Esteem with a Friend's Help

Find one friend whom you can trust and who is interested in supporting you. You must be prepared to accept both support and criticism from that friend. Ask your friend to spend one hour a day with you for thirty days just listening to you talk about your day and your general feelings about life.

During the first week, ask your friend not to respond to what you say until the very end of the week. Tell her that you want her to answer the following questions at the end of the first week:

- Do I exaggerate the negative or positive parts of myself?
- Do I exaggerate the negative or positive parts of others?
- Am I as hard on others as I am on myself?
- Am I perfectionistic, expecting things to go exactly as I pictured them and being disappointed if they don't follow that course 100 percent?
- Do I tend to expect things to turn out badly?

- Do I project that I am unlovable?
- Do I complain a lot?
- Do I want everyone to change but me?
- Am I willing to do anything in order to keep someone in my life?
- Do I see every challenge as a crisis?

At the end of the first week, answer these questions about yourself on a sheet of paper and ask your friend to do the same. Compare lists. Use her list and select one characteristic that you wish to change. Let's say that it's exaggerating the negative parts of yourself. Both of you will then concentrate only on that issue the following week. Each day when you are with your friend, list a number of negative comments that you make about yourself at the end of the hour. Your friend will make a statement to you about the validity of what you say on the basis of what she already knows about you.

Here's how it might go:

You: Men don't like me.
Her: Come on. You've been married once, engaged once and dated six men in the last year. Men like you.
You: That's true, but the men I like don't like me.

Her: You never tell the men you like that you care about them. Why would you expect them to tell you?

You: I told Peter I liked him and he never asked me out again.

Her: Maybe Peter is shy or thought you might be ready for a serious romance. In any case, the one man you told you liked didn't stick around. That's a lot different from saying "All men don't like me." Maybe you say that to protect yourself, but it's also going to keep you from meeting men.

There's no question that this kind of alliance asks a lot of a friendship, but it can make a real difference in your life if a friend will stick it out for four weeks.

During the third week, your friend can begin to make positive suggestions about things that you can do differently. Here's where your courage comes in. Because you've already entrusted this friend with some of your deepest thoughts and fears, this is the time to have the courage to take the risk of making some small changes that the two of you can monitor together.

In the fourth week, the two of you should assess what has been going on over the last three weeks, what changes you can see in yourself and whether the friendship can tolerate going back over the list of questions and finding another area for self-improvement.

If you discover that your original negative self-esteem list contains so many problem areas that no one friend can help you work them all out, then you may need to consider professional help.

Professional Help in Building Self-Esteem

Any woman who knows in her heart that she did not have a loving childhood relationship with her mother, or who still cannot communicate with her mother in a kind, respectful and sensitive way, would do herself a great service if she worked with a female counselor. It could be a major step in providing her with a positive female role model.

I feel that the support and affection of a well-balanced, good-humored, insightful female therapist is critical in helping women first to see themselves as worthy and then to move out into the world to find worthy male partners. Why do I insist on a woman to help you to maturity? Because so many of us have been deprived of love by our mothers. A female therapist can offer a therapeutic alliance, becoming a surrogate parent, someone you respect, admire and have a continuing relationship with, whom you can continually go back to for a tuneup. This can be your "good mother" and can provide the missing link to a new opportunity for enhanced self-esteem. It is of major importance to select a female mentor who is healthy, who likes herself, who may herself have suffered through personal turmoil and come out of it able to give and accept love, someone who can care about you and show you that you are lovable. A female therapist offers you the opportunity to form a warm relationship with an autonomous, noncompetitive woman who is involved in your life for *your* sake. She can therefore help you to love the right men and to choose the mate who is best for you.

Building self-esteem requires tiny steps forward and every step is important, every effort counts. If we want love, we first need trust and acceptance from someone who will love us as we are, tell us so, then help us become more. Such a relationship offers a chance to let go of unpleasant memories of disappointing past loves and allows us the proof that we're lovable and capable of giving love in return.

For years, a woman's only option in therapy was to try to find herself worthy as a female by seeking out a male therapist. But our initial love object in life is a female, and if we cannot fix things ourselves or with a friend, often just a few sessions with a warm, loving woman will help us to get back on track, to see that women can be competent, loving and lovable. It can make a major difference in breaking down the negative messages from the past.

4

Getting the Crumbs Out of Bed

The Crumbs Women Bring to Marriage

"This time the call came at 11:30," Mattie told me. "I didn't want to go, but I *did.*"

Mattie sat in my office teary-eyed, relating a story I'd heard before during the year she'd been seeing me for therapy. Her boyfriend, Bob, was treating her badly— only now it was worse. She didn't know if she could endure it much longer, or if she could endure life without him.

Mattie is a voluptuous blond, and she plays up her sexiness. Bob adores her, or more accurately, he adores her body. In the last few months, he's made it clear that's all he wants from her. He calls her late at night, and in his huskiest voice asks her to come over. For four years she's been dragging herself out of bed and driving over to see him through rain, snow or sleet, only to disrobe, get into bed with him and enjoy "frantic, reckless" sex. When it's over, Bob whispers, "You know how I hate to sleep with someone. I'll call you tomorrow."

Mattie gets out of bed feeling sexually spent and, as she closes Bob's door, she also feels more depressed and lonely than before the call. Yet she wants to keep on seeing him. Sex with Bob does something to her— it's exciting, unlike the sex she had with her husband when she was married. But Bob is a real crumb!

And then there's Sandra, a twenty-eight-year-old schoolteacher who married two years ago. She was a virgin when she became Paul's wife—and he liked that about her. Paul is a lawyer, thirty-five years old and highly sexed. In fact, he's a man who's perpetually turned on. He demands sex from Sandra twice a day during the week and three times daily on weekends. She's in pain, literally, physically and emotionally. She's developed a bladder infection and the doctor has ordered her to not have sex until it clears. For the first time in a long time, she doesn't have to deal with Paul's insistent passion.

"What do I do now?" she asks me. "When the infection is gone, I'll have to go back to the routine.

Sex two and three times a day. I can't bear the thought of it anymore."

Sandra is worried about refusing Paul or revealing her disdain for such excessive sex. During their first year of marriage, she turned him down, begging him to leave her alone for a few days. A story got back to her that during his first marriage Paul's wife refused sex and he took up with someone else. What's Sandra to do? She doesn't want to have sex with him with such frequency, but she doesn't dare refuse him. He'll go elsewhere and perhaps leave her.

Both of these women bring crumbs from the past into their sex lives—they are living with attitudes they learned in childhood and have not yet given up.

Sex Is Best When It's Taboo

Mattie's dilemma is that she has separated sex from love, and finds true excitement in sex only when it's taboo. Bob is not only an extramarital lover, but he summons her like a sheik to his tent, then dismisses her when he's had his pleasure. Mattie's excited and degraded at the same time. The crumb she brings to her bed is giving sex an inflated meaning in an atmosphere that has no mutual respect. She's the "bad" girl with a worse man.

No wonder Bob treats Mattie badly. He never has

to be really intimate with her. He never has to worry about getting beyond the sexual side of the relationship. He never has to deal with a real person, just with her body, because that's the way she negotiates with the world.

What reward does Mattie get from going to Bob in the middle of the night? She must take a rational look at the advantages and disadvantages of giving him up. Does he enhance her self-esteem? No. Is he a friend, an ally, a protector when she leaves in the early hours of the night? No. More important, she uses her sexual attachment to Bob to put off finding a long-term relationship in which she might develop emotional rapport. Intimacy terrifies her.

Mattie thinks of herself as having an "affair," though it's actually sex on demand. But to her, an affair in itself is exciting. Sex in a passionate affair can never be compared to sex in marriage or any relationship in which two people are not always accessible to each other and always leave each other half-satisfied. In marriage, you may feel trapped or obligated, or as if you have a duty or are a possession. In an affair, you can spend half the week preparing for an evening of "love," and the other half reminiscing. In marriage, you try your best to bring renewed pleasure to bed night after night, but it may be increasingly difficult for the woman who finds taboo sex more delectable.

Getting rid of the crumbs takes a little rational thought. It takes understanding that socially sanctioned relationships and sex go together. It's not only okay, but terrific to enjoy sex with someone you like and love, and who loves you in return. That's certainly preferable to sex with a man who'd send you out into the night and turn his back on you.

Sex Is a Duty for a Good Girl

Sandra is caught between the teachings of a stringent moral background and the lascivious demands of the husband she loves. The crumbs she brings to her marriage bed are as weighty as Mattie's and they are sugar-coated with a commitment to virtue as well. Sandra is the "good girl," a virgin when she married, who came from a home that discouraged any demonstration or discussion of sexuality. Sex was defined as unpleasant and repulsive. Her mother told her to "bear up" and "endure."

Among other outdated notions, Sandra was taught that a good girl doesn't respond too energetically in bed. The reasoning was that it might upset her husband—he'll worry that if she's "hot," she'll be prone to adultery. This logic escapes anyone except the people who for some unknown reason perpetuate it. And it follows that if good girls don't initiate sex, they don't refuse it either. Good girls do their duty. Sandra actually found herself liking sex when she was first married, but the frequency put her off. She didn't know that other women don't experience such activity, and since she was shy and wouldn't talk about sex, she assumed she was just one of millions of other women "bearing up" under this carnal burden.

To sweep these crumbs out of her bed and save herself body and spirit, Sandra must confront Paul. *She must change.* All her experiences have brought her to this point. Now she must clear the bed she's lying in and decide if Paul is the man she'll choose to stay there with. She has a few choices: She can attempt to make this a more equitable, less sexually demanding marriage, she can help Paul to make *his* adjustments or she can leave.

Sandra is willing to negotiate. If Paul doesn't find the new Sandra to be romantic, *he* will have to deal with that. Sandra has determined what she thinks is a desirable number of times for sex—perhaps alternate days of the week. No more sex on demand. Sandra will have to rehearse a dialogue with Paul and prepare for all his rationalizations. If she can open the discussion by saying, "I love you, Paul, but we need to come to an agreement about sex. What is reasonable for you?" she's already made a significant change. She is suggesting that she wants to cooperate, not deny or begrudge, and that she wants to get some pleasure out of their sexual encounters. If he insists that he must have sex twice a day, Sandra can suggest an alternative to intercourse: Masturbation also provides him with an outlet.

Most married people practice masturbation at one time or another—it's not a perversion or an unusual occurrence. Nor does it condemn the wife whose husband does it. In Sandra's case, it's a matter of taking a risk and suggesting it—feeling assured she won't be abandoned if she turns her husband down for sex.

Sex Is a Weapon

Karen told me that in the 1960s she participated in an "encounter group" experiment in which the object was to "get in touch with her feelings." One exercise involved all the eighteen people in the group holding hands and standing in a circle. Karen, the first player, was to stand outside the circle and try to break in by using any device she wanted except violence. She could push, wheedle, cajole, argue, bargain or try to pry interlocking fingers apart.

Karen said her solution was very simple and came to her immediately. She walked over to the most attractive man in the group and began stroking his back, nuzzling his neck. Her ploy was to seduce him just enough—to excite him to the point at which his grip on his neighbor's hand was loosened and she could break through. Her attempt worked.

Karen said it surprised her that she immediately tried seduction as a means of "belonging." It didn't go along with her image of herself—she wasn't a woman who used sex to get what she wanted from men. Or was she? When she thought about it, using seductiveness made sense: It was the path of least resistance to most men. And if she could disarm them, why not? Being honest with herself, she could see how she had used sex in her first marriage. It failed because both she and her husband used sex to fool each other into believing they "belonged together" or to get what they wanted from each other.

George was sexually demanding of Karen and she was completely responsive in the beginning—she loved being desired so fervently. He became possessive of her and unfaithful at the same time. After a year of marriage, he'd withhold sex from her if he was angry; she took her turn and did the same with him.

Three years later, she and George weren't sleeping together any longer. Karen tried to seduce him back to loving her, desiring her, but it didn't work.

Nothing backfires as quickly or as hurtfully in a marriage as using sex as a weapon or for gain. *The Total Woman* preached at-home randy behavior to seduce a husband into doling out material favors ("I put on a sheer apron, a string of pearls, and nothing else and got the coat I wanted next day"), as if it were a charming virtue to prostitute yourself every time you saw something you wanted in a store. If a couple agrees that an exchange of sex is worth a fur wrap or a dinette set, so be it. Fortunately, most of us don't exercise such contempt for the men we love or for ourselves.

Sex has always been used as a commodity, and no one knows this better than the women who use their bodies not only to get clothing and gems, but also for power positions at work. Even in marriage, sex can be a tool in the game of "who's topping whom." A patient of mine has been married to a man who works diligently, she says, at helping her have an orgasm. But she hasn't, not once in fifteen years of marriage. One thing that puts her off is his nightly comment, hundreds of variations on, "Well, perhaps tonight you'll have an orgasm!" The challenge stops her cold. He may say it to her over dinner, as they're undressing, whenever he chooses. She stiffens. He wants her to have an orgasm, but pretty much tells her she won't and thus exerts his total power over her.

In Karen's case, sex became the only bond between her and George. It was the one thing they had together and they denied it to each other in playing their individual power games. Both shared a "crumb," an idea that sex is a tool and that it is the only way to achieve lasting love. And when Karen didn't get what she wanted emotionally from George, she didn't have to think very fast to come up with something that might hurt him.

What are the advantages of using sex as a weapon? For some women, sex is the only power they've got in the relationship. Their bodies are their own—they can achieve pleasure through them or deny pleasure with them. They may be controlled or temporarily hurt by a man, but unless they agree to it, they will not be penetrated by a man.

To get this crumb out of bed, Karen and women like her must confront their anger and express what's bothering them, as thinking, adult women. The connection between sex and anger is real—women tend to withhold sex when they're angry and often even when a fight's resolved. Men may not withhold sex when they're angry and often need the reassurance of sex after a fight. They feel that sex is the fastest way to reestablish the bond. They may not be able to say, "I'm sorry," but they use lovemaking to express it. Can the relationship be healed without using sex as a tool? Does a man actually understand what he's doing to displease a woman? Sex between two caring people is one of life's great pleasures. It's sad to think of it used as if it were a cold, manipulative weapon.

The Crumbs Men Bring to Marriage

Male and female dynamics differ in a number of ways, but like women, men bring their own crumbs into relationships. Each brings a certain personal history, preconditioned attitudes about women, that have been with him most of his life.

The Separation of Sex and Love

Men think in terms of potency, power, domination, pursuit and conquest when they define sexuality. That puts a lot of pressure on one simple physical act. But they also need tenderness, a safe place wherein they can be vulnerable, protected, cherished—qualities they connect with love. It's male biology—millions of years old and still a bit primitive—that encourages the need to dominate, and it exerts the greatest pull between men and women at first. It's biology that gets men interested in women, but it's socialization, the need for protection, that determines how interested he will be and how he shows it.

Men have learned to separate sex from love. It's a trait stemming from basic biology and conditioning. It often gets them into trouble. They can more easily distance themselves emotionally from women during sex, or they can more easily be unfaithful in a marriage.

This ability to separate the two may answer the question: Why do men like sex after a fight? With some men, sex is the only way they know to recapture intimacy. Even though sex after quarreling has hostile underpinnings, at another level it's rather a tender mercy—sex is the only way they can get close to a woman. For others, sex on the heels of an out-and-out blowup just reinforces their sense of control and domination. But for the man who's basically good-hearted, if confused, lovemaking allows a woman to show him forgiveness. It's all he wants: Forgive him and let him go on with his life!

His Mother, Your Mother-in-Law

A man's attitudes about women have always been influenced by his relationship with his mother. The big question, of course, is, Who was she to him? He may have perceived her as saintly—a very good woman, of impeccable virtue, self-sacrificing, someone who lived for the children. She may have been cold and distant, seductive, threatening or harsh. Or his mother could have been wholesome and loving, protective and good-humored, everyone's "ideal" mother.

Maybe she told him all women are seductresses, ego inflaters, or opportunists. She may have overindulged him, sending him out into the world totally unprepared to deal with women who won't, as she did, provide everything he needs. Was he a child of divorce, raised by his mother? She may have ruled him in ways that suppressed some of his normal masculine instincts, particularly if she had a bias against men. Her target may have been his playfulness, self-assertion, aggression or ambition.

There's no rule that dictates how a man will interact with you because of his mother's influence, but studies show there are a number of predictable behavior patterns. If he adores his mother and sees her as saintly or overly dominating, be prepared not to have sex with him too frequently—what he demands of saints is chastity. If he sees her as an overbearing witch, he won't touch you, because he'll see you in the same way. He may initiate premarital sex, but expect his ardor to diminish once you're married. It will be noticeable, too. Whatever passion remains after a few children arrive can dwindle to very little sexual contact. If a woman takes on the role of mother too wholeheartedly, she often forgets about being a loving, sensual being to a man. Pure "mother" status may also free her from an obligation for marital sex, and the husband who wants a saintly wife may be relieved by this turn of events. A woman's motherliness can touch off incestuous feelings he harbors for his own mother, causing him anxiety. So the asexual wife is perfect for him. He can even tomcat around to get his needs met elsewhere, if he's so inclined. At home, the wife-mother basically supervises his life, raises model children, and keeps the home fires stoked. But to have sex, he makes a phone call to a different woman.

This crumb leaves some dusty debris if a man develops a madonna/prostitute complex because of his saintly mother. If he divides all women into these two types, it will pose a serious dilemma for a woman who's "good" and cares to be sexual. She'll be "bad" in his eyes.

"Good girl/bad girl" beliefs mean not only that the good girl *doesn't* and the bad girl *does,* but also that the good girl doesn't connect sex with pleasure and the bad girl doesn't connect sex with self-esteem. The good girl/madonna is respectable—everyone assumes she went to the altar pure, anticipating only the sexual joys her husband would bring to her. The young husband believes, on principle, that madonnas feel only spiritual ecstasy, so he won't be surprised when his wife is reluctant to have sex—or proves herself either passionless or asexual. Sexual ecstasy, by mutual agreement, is exclusively his and forbidden to her. When she ponders sexuality, the madonna may feel irrational guilt and block her own impulses, flipping a switch into stern self-denial. Sex is for procreation and therein lies her pleasure—there will be an end result from carnal pleasures, a baby. Satisfying a man, giving him pleasure, is incidental. If a man knows his basically nonsexual wife already feels used or put upon during straight sex, he won't tell her about his secret fantasies. For him to express them without permission would humiliate her, but to get her permission, he has to talk about them and perhaps humiliate himself.

A man with a hostile mother is more likely to have a taste for sexual selfishness and even marital rape. With this guy, the only free will is *his*—he's free to take his pleasure and his wife's not free to say no. Sex is power to such a frightened male, who exerts dominance by translating his rape-and-rapture fantasies into near-violent acts. Rape punishes a wife, degrades her, reinforces his sadistic reasoning. Women, he thinks, are *bad* to begin with—like his mother—and *very* bad for arousing him.

The man with a depriving, critical mother will have sex to procreate, or to keep a woman satisfied enough so she doesn't seek another man's company. When he wants to indulge himself without restraint, he seeks other women. Of his many fears, one stands out: He fears he'll never satisfy her in many ways—whatever money he makes will not be enough, whatever position he attains professionally will be inadequate, however much he desires her, she'll laugh at him. This man is always proving himself, and when he seeks another woman, she is likely to be someone who accepts him unconditionally.

Marriage can release the worst in a man like this. He's oversensitive to any slightly negative observation or comment. If he feels he's not fulfilling a wife in any number of ways, he may set up an insurmountable barrier to intimacy—ignoring her totally, for example. He becomes angry if she feels helpless and is unable to break through his barriers. At the same time, he resents having to put the barriers there in the first place! It's hard to get anywhere with this man. The woman who lives with him can't be open. A vicious circle is perpetuated between them.

Communication is argumentative, even when the moment calls for tenderness. For example, a husband buys his wife a present. Her response is, "It's very nice, John, I appreciate it, but I'll tell you the truth— I'd have preferred . . . " John is offended. He can't say, "If that's what you want, I'm happy to get it for you!" Instead, he presumes her request for something different is a value judgment against him and his masculinity: "Don't expect me to buy you anything again," he warns her.

If he wants more sex, he'll ask for it outright: "Let's have sex." If she answers, "I'm sorry, not tonight. Please understand," he turns his back on her, wounded and angry. "Next time you want sex," he pouts, "you'll have to ask me and maybe I'll think about it." This man is hypersensitive. He was childlike going into the marriage and he hasn't grown since. Their argumentative relationship develops from unresolved disappointments with each other and an inability to talk things out.

Taboo and Not Taboo

Before a couple marries their sex is often playful and exciting, with various sensuous games acted out to please each other. After marriage, the man usually assumes that he'll introduce experimental sex into the relationship. He's feeling more comfortable with his wife, so why not? But many a man discovers a conflict about now: His wife is too accessible! What inflamed him was the *fight* for her—the heat of sex outside marriage. He may have fantasies about sex with her, but he draws back from her. Suddenly, he feels more vulnerable than masterful. What's happened between them? For this man, sex is most exciting when it's taboo. This repressive sexual attitude is still an issue between couples in the very sophisticated 1980s.

Call it old-fashioned, but sex outside marriage has an element of anticipatory passion and excitement, an extra *frisson*. In marriage, there's not only open access to each other, there's also the expectation of open access, the legal assurance of open access, the moral injunction, in effect, to do your *duty*. Men talk about marital obligations to their wives. Women discuss marital obligations to their husbands. They may remember the early passion, but now they sleep back to back— wondering if they'll ever recapture the high sexual spirit of courtship. In marriage, the ambiance of sex has changed. A man's urges can be squelched by something as simple as familiarity with a woman who's no longer forbidden.

Sex as Power

Not all men would admit to this when questioned, and some won't let themselves believe it even in the privacy of their own thoughts: Women don't know the power of their own sexuality and how it affects men! Sex has great power. Men have started wars over women, composed masterpieces of poetry and music to celebrate the joy of love; they've given themselves over to causes great and small to satisfy a passion. Men have walked out of marriages for women who weren't their intellectual equals or who weren't capable of caring for them on the most basic levels. What they succumbed to was the power of sex and how they felt with the woman who gave herself to him—they felt triumphant, potent and alive!

As much as men love sex at this level of intensity,

they also fear that it will dominate their lives in counterproductive ways. So a man who is moved by sex with a particular woman may also try to distance himself from her. He's afraid she will distract him from his work, divert his ambitions; that any gesture she makes, no matter how innocent, will be the catalyst of his downfall. He doesn't want to be *obsessed* with her, because she is someone he could lose himself in— a sexually intriguing person.

Shere Hite, in *The Hite Report,* made a fascinating point: She said that men who were strivers—ambitious, driven men—did not get involved with women who they knew would have too profound an effect on them. They chose *not* to marry women they loved with passion or abandon, but to wed *safer* women whom they cared about but who would not distract them. Another survey, done by authors Francis Bremer and Emily Vogel for their book *Coping With His Success,* noted that 67 percent of women married to very successful men reported unsatisfactory sex lives. One reason is that physical and psychological energy is diverted into working. These men sublimate sex drive into professional channels.

A man's self-worth is inextricably tied to his success in the world. If he's successful in his career, he is a *man*. Society doesn't describe manhood in terms of a satisfactory interpersonal relationship with a woman! It defines manhood or masculinity as power-centered—"Love 'em or leave 'em." Women with sexual power can intimidate such a man. And rather than embracing a woman in a healthy interdependency, he may develop tremendous fears of the woman to whom he's most attracted.

Attractive women are the ones most likely to make him aware of his sexual vulnerability. He's afraid that he'll be destroyed by a seductive woman. He just cannot think of her or touch her without feeling he'll lose control. This man *must* have the power and call the shots. If he feels threatened or anxious, he'll try to defuse her seductive power by intimidating her and making sure she won't be sexually available to him.

The relationship between sex and power has another aspect too: One reason virgin status is so sought after and cherished by men is that a woman can then be overcome by male sexuality. Since a virgin has no one to compare him to—the size of his penis, his technique, his endurance—the first lover is the master. A virgin is an innocent, to be schooled by one man in what will please him.

Men are different in style, tempo and disposition, and this doesn't make them superior or inferior—just different. But in one way they are alike—most need to feel they have most of the power in sexual encounters. A woman with sexual power may suffer for it at the hands of a man who's unhealthy. Or, if she finds the right man, one who accepts her sexuality, she'll have a better chance of getting the crumbs out of *her* bed.

How Women and Men Can Both Get the Crumbs Out of Bed: A Four-Part Lesson

Dusting away the crumbs isn't as easy as making a swiping gesture, but keep that image in mind—it will be useful. Getting the crumbs out of bed involves re-education—a wiping away of outdated attitudes and feelings about sex.

Begin by giving yourself permission to be a sexual person. If you've come to the marriage bed from a non–permission-giving environment, one that perpetuated the madonna/prostitute complex or the sex-is-better-when-it's-taboo philosophy, accept that you are a sensate being who can give herself entirely. Sex is interesting when you explore it with someone you love, and not a choice between good and bad. Do some rational thinking: Ask yourself if having sex with a person you care for makes you a bad person. The only answer is no!

Give yourself permission to tell the other person what is and what isn't appealing to you about sex. A patient told me that she and her husband had almost no sex life for about six months. Finally, he told her what the problem was: She'd gained nearly forty pounds since their marriage. "I didn't marry a fat girl," he told her, "and I find you unattractive. The way you look is important to me and once you looked great. But don't ask me to feel sexual toward you when you're in this shape!" He also told her, "I'm telling you how I feel and you can decide what to do."

Was he cruel to say this? Not really. In fact, he's taken a first step in getting a crumb out of bed—his wife's carelessness about her body. Will she lose weight? She will, or lose *him*.

A precursor to lovemaking explains the other side of this: Let people know what it is you like about them. Draw them closer with sincere observations and compliments about how they look, dress, are stylish. Connect to others. Sex begins the moment you walk through the door—not when a hand touches your body.

Give yourself permission to ask the person you love to help you. Sex is an integral part of a relationship. That means there's someone there to care about you. Care about them, too, and let them in on any problem-solving you want to do. They are feeling the irritation from the "crumbs," too, so let them help you dust them away. Ask for tenderness. Ask for time as you work toward solutions. Invite your mate to help you. The other person may have just the right knack for putting you on a bed of roses.

Give yourself permission to reach a balanced relationship with generous love and warm sex. A balanced relationship means you can desire a person and on occasion feel you *need* that person—and that's okay. A balanced relationship is love and sex, enjoying the other person for more than what he or she contributes to it. If a relationship revolves around crumbly ideals from the past, played out again and again, there can only be resounding disappointment. Give yourself permission to *grow!*

How We Make Our Beds Uncomfortable

Those who enjoy sex most are people who've got a good sense of self-esteem—who aren't desperate to connect with another, who are capable of a positive exchange and don't use sex as a tool, as a way of gaining power. Sex is best because they know what it *is*. It doesn't have to involve moving mountains with each kiss or end with the ultimate orgasm!

The woman who is a healthy lover knows sex has a strong emotional component that makes her feel good about herself—she can give and receive. The healthy sexual woman isn't merely goal-oriented—needing to reach orgasm (or fake it) one or more times to feed tender male egos that must prove themselves through sexual prowess. The healthy male understands that he can get pleasure when his lover has pleasure, without being sexually demanding or setting unreachable goals for her to meet. Both are comfortable touching and being touched.

Sex changes with familiarity, and the pattern of sexual behavior is very consistent in relationships. Though no two are identical, the ones that fail usually exhibit a predictable cycle with respect to sex.

Intensity of sexuality: A couple just getting to know each other experience lavish, tension-ridden, splendidly energetic and fulfilling sexual episodes. Newness creates excitement—there's passion in overcoming barriers, conquering and being conquered. Each partner is committed to satisfying the other, reassuring the other of his or her desirability and lovability. With romanticism comes flash fighting, indulgence of whims, even moodiness as both wonder if this will last. Yet each thinks the other is *perfect* at this point. They believe the union is precious and they savor every moment together.

Establishment of care and trust: No longer taboo, sex is sanctioned by marriage or an agreement between the couple to be faithful to each other. Sex cools down a bit, and it's normal to have pleasant, comfortable, satisfying sexual experiences rather than extreme sexual highs. Many women who are slightly inhibited before marriage or commitment may lose inhibitions as they feel trust in a partner and the assurance of continuity. They're still interested in pleasing each other, but they know the chase is basically over and unchallenged love sustains them. At this point, partners begin to notice frailties—each becomes more endearingly human.

Conflicts between sex and love: Conflicts that separate sex from love are a normal occurrence for most couples. A man with a poor sense of himself, for example, may not be able to join with a woman in a long-term loving relationship—and time informs him of this all too harshly. If there are children, the couple's sex life typically diminishes. Statistics tell us that with each child, couples have less time or inclination for mutual pleasure. Familiarity can dampen a man's interest in his wife, and a wife's attraction to her husband. Nothing she does surprises and delights him; and, in turn, she won't improvise and tantalize him in ways that please him. She may have used sex to tempt him into a marriage he didn't want in the first place. If he feels threatened by her sexuality, a husband may resent his wife's efforts to initiate sex. He'll strike out against her, blaming her for his problems—sexual or otherwise.

Loving and being loved—understanding what love is—is a daily concern for everyone. Sex is an important part of loving, but it's a fringe benefit. Some people argue that a good sexual relationship is possible *without* a good emotional relationship. Conversely, others hold that if sex doesn't work for a couple, it means nothing is worth having or building on in that relationship. And studies show that many couples live in relative marital satisfaction with no sexual contact. Nothing is true for everyone. What *is* true is that couples will reach a point at which they question how they feel about intimacy and desire. Can they integrate love and sex the way they did early on in the relationship? They begin to worry about this, and this may lead to . . .

Lack of communication and lack of spontaneity: Even good relationships can eventually suffer from a distancing as each partner involves himself or herself in the process of living—the complications of living with someone *and* making a living. Careers interfere with caring for each other. Problems mount, are unmentioned. A marital style starts to take hold. A man relegates his woman to the "little wife" status, and blights the relationship by diminishing her. A wife, fearing that the relationship is suffering, flatters her husband falsely—wanting him to be greater than he is, trying to make him a hero. A husband needs his wife to be the anchor that holds down one corner of his world while he tries to make it out there. Sexually, they probably are not in synch. What's happening here?

By letting problems mount and not discussing them in rational, constructive ways, couples can fall into bad bedroom habits. The relationship is running on misunderstandings. Each feels overly sensitive to the other's criticism and say nothing about the *real* issues, and the partners start sniping at each other. Neither has found the energy or inclination to reappraise their goals, state their problems and plan solutions openly and honestly. They live like two people facing each other in a rowboat, looking over each other's shoulder and not telling the other what the view is!

A love relationship is a voluntary, continuing commitment. It involves the recognition that someone can be with you but also has the choice to be *without* you. Relationship by invitation, not obligation, allows itself to be renewed on a daily basis: "I love you and I want this relationship to work." When union is by obligation, problems go unsolved because of admonitions, predictable emotional game-playing, threats—the old "crumbs." Relationship by obligation also provides lots of opportunities for empty promises: "Promise me you'll never say that again," "Promise me you'll buy me that sofa if we have sex tonight." And the problems in this kind of relationship won't be solved by suggesting unlimited freedom and little obligation: "Do what you want to do," "I don't mind if you see other women as long as I know you come home to me." Open marriage may work temporarily to release tension, but it's not in the best interest of either partner or the relationship. Basic values get lost within a trendy and impractical solution, and the partners end by resenting each other.

An ideal relationship is a bit more difficult to reach, but it's worth striving for. To get the crumbs of the past out of bed, take a look at what you carry into your marriage from generations past. Look at your vocabulary. Do you speak in exaggerated terms? Do you *hate* everything about your mate, are you always *beside yourself* or *wiped out,* or are you *mad* for him, *crazy* in love, *breathless?* Do you expect your partner to fit these descriptions or think he has no effect on you unless the effect is extreme? Do you have explosive exchanges over minor points, fighting for every breath, every bit of power? Do you find you are disruptive just to get attention from a partner? Is tender affection part of you, part of him? Are you able to give each other affection—giving, not giving in?

Relationship by invitation, not obligation, wields the greatest force. It does not take love for granted! It values every moment love is exchanged between two people. Of all crimes of the heart, none is so common as assuming that we have a right to love and be loved by the person we're joined to, whether they like it or not. Take love for granted and it can slip away. You'll know if you've taken love for granted if you fear you cannot ask your mate: "Would you marry me again?" "Do you like coming home at night?" "Am I lovable?" "What are some of the things that I can do to improve this relationship?" If the question you want to ask is, "Don't I have a right to lifetime support, companionship, fidelity and sexual cooperation?" you place your relationship in jeopardy—it will crumble!

The chances of a relationship working depend on the degree of emotional stability and maturity of both partners. You have to work for fulfillment. It's not a gift. Dreaming makes us lazy. You need to work on yourself before starting a relationship, then work for a relationship that can stand the test of time. A good one requires a balance between forgoing and granting, between restrictions and freedom, between feeling a loss of control over yourself and needing control of others, giving tender affection and being appropriately assertive when hurt. It's the pleasure of knowing you are both *reunited,* happily, on a daily basis . . . and that there's not one crumb in sight!

5

From Cream Puff to Tart

OFFICIALLY, it was a group of friends having a lunch. But midway through the poached salmon, it turned into a personal drama that reflected the recent history of the women's movement. No one expected this occurrence, least of all the hostess—a woman known for her cool, a self-made millionaire by the age of thirty-six, and for the first time in nine years alone, since her husband's departure six months before.

Eight women friends sat around the table, each an achiever in her own way. Among them were three businesswomen, a doctor, an actress, a screenwriter, a columnist for a midwestern newspaper and a commercial artist. One of them had been profiled in a national magazine, another was well-known locally, all of them earned good incomes at careers they liked. Two were married.

The hostess, who'd made her money by some infallible instinct for stock-market sure things, answered one of her guests' questions about how she was faring since her husband had left. "I'll be just fine," Kate said quietly. "Nine years of marriage, gone. I can't believe it." Her voice was shaky, but she smiled valiantly.

Fran, a high-powered businesswoman, admired the view from the restaurant window and added, "At least Hal didn't take your business with him. Or the apartment."

"Wrecking your business is grounds for murder," Toby put in. She was Kate's childhood friend from Louisiana, divorced and the mother of four children, an entrepreneur who'd turned her father's small neighborhood bakery into a successful catering concern.

"Where would we be without our careers?" someone asked.

"Let's count our blessings," Fran said. "Even if one of them isn't a guy and we made deals for the rest." She lifted her glass. Most of the women laughed because they understood the machinations that had been necessary to get and keep a career. For six of them, there was no man to share the bounty.

"I killed myself to make it," Dee said. She was the

actress, enjoying recent popularity. "I don't want to lose it, ever."

They all toasted careers in perpetuity.

"We're amazing," Toby said. "We know how to get what we want. We know how to make money . . . more money than most men. Dee's getting a million bucks for a movie, Fran's about to buy a plane, for heaven's sake!" She continued around the table, enumerating triumphs.

And right about here, Kate broke down. She complimented the other women on their successes, then confessed to the group that she was not like them at all—she was an imposter, and they'd know it soon because when Hal left, he took her heart *and* her ambition with him. "I want my husband back," she cried. "I want my old life again. I made it all for *him,* for *us.*"

Everyone jumped to comfort her. They assured Kate she was experiencing the classic emotional exhaustion that accompanies divorce. She'd soon meet another man, they told her, someone finer. Meanwhile, hadn't she managed to pull off a financial coup in the middle of a grisly property settlement? She didn't need Hal to function superlatively. Wasn't that proof enough?

Without Hal, Kate replied, her accomplishments were meaningless. With him, they counted. Without him, she could no longer acknowledge her abilities, her humor, her talent or her strengths. They were simply quirks of personality. With Hal, she was dynamic, clever, unselfish. Without a man, her business and the energy she'd put into it were little more than unrelated scraps of paper.

"Does anyone know what I'm talking about?" Kate looked at us all for acknowledgment. "Are we all so tough?" She hesitated a moment, then added, "I curse my father for telling me to go into business. Why did I listen to him? Why didn't I see it would destroy me?"

I was among Kate's luncheon guests and I heard her questions. We all knew exactly what she was talking about so passionately. We had, each of us, felt the same way in our own lives. We all identified with her ambivalence about pursuing careers and being autonomous, battling with the urge to give up professional goals and surrender to traditional roles. Kate wasn't just telling us that her life had diminished when Hal departed—it was something more critical: Kate is a woman in conflict, like many others. The issue is no longer "Can we get the jobs?" but why we feel that getting the job is synonymous with losing the man. Kate needed the balance between love and work *less than* she needed love to sugar-coat her estimable ambition. She loved Hal, but the truth was she loved work more—and it scared her. The more her ambition scared her, the more she made Hal her reason for living.

Kate is suffering from one of modern woman's real dilemmas: How does a woman who is ambitious and successful strike a balance between love and work? How does she justify success to herself? Can she succeed without feeling guilty about achieving? Must she find solace in downplaying her accomplishments, demeaning her own impulses toward building or sustaining a career, and bitterly blaming another for having encouraged her in the first place—as if she were the unwitting victim of her mentor? Must relationships suffer when women have careers?

A husband comes in handy to absorb some of the pressures of being a striving woman. He has to be a remarkable fellow, too—neither desperately counting the ways in which she's outpacing him professionally, or economically, or both, nor plotting strategies to keep her emotionally dependent, sabotaging her efforts so she'll need his support. He has to have a measure of self-confidence. The partner of a woman who's proved she can "take charge" has to exude at least an equal amount of power. And though he may be a freshly minted New Man willing to confess to frailty and not feel emasculated or pitiable, he often harbors a traditional streak. So it was with Hal.

He needed the balm of "wifeliness" from Kate. It

soothed them both, even if being wifely meant little more than ladling out a bowl of soup. During those moments both played traditional roles, but over dinner they also discussed plans for spending and having. And while it was Kate who had the advantage of money, it was Hal for whom the "sacrifices" were made: "I'm doing it for us . . . Hal thinks big . . . Hal wants a summer house . . . Hal thinks we need a better address."

Kate was ambitious, but Hal was, too, and she coached him in how to wheel and deal as she'd been taught by her father. He never surpassed her. She proved her skills in a field dominated by men and this, deep down, always frightened her. It touched on the conflict between her emotional and practical definitions of femininity: Emotionally, she could downplay her success and ascribe it to the *luck* factor—as five out of ten top women executives did in *Savvy* magazine, speaking of their own successes. But her practical definition allowed for competence, intelligence, goal-setting and courage enriched by coexistence with "feminine" needs for a home, security, love.

Kate believed that with her husband gone, attitudes toward her would change. People would still tell her she was everything they wanted to be, still ask her for guidance, but in her heart she would know they were laughing at her for failing at the most basic task— holding on to a man.

Kate's problem is one that many of us can relate to, and so is that of Judith, a patient of mine. She faces the career woman's other dilemma: In setting up their lives so that ambitions come first, many women meet the challenges in the tough business world, hold titles and make deals, but they are lonely, frustrated, in emotional isolation. When business becomes the first priority, love suffers. As ambition grows, the need for relationships is soon *denied.* Love takes up too much room for these women; they turn off to intimacy and pursue gratification through positioning at the office. Judith's story describes what can happen when a cream puff becomes a tart!

She was known as the woman who could wear an ice cube fixed on a chain around her neck and take it off at the end of the day, still intact, all edges sharp, with no sign of melting. She knew what others thought of her, but pretended it didn't matter. She had the corner office, with a view; the others didn't. *Cool* got her the kind of position only nine or ten other women in the country held; warmth had kept her in the steno pool for seven low-paying but eventful years.

That's where Judith began—as a secretary. "I never thought of myself as a career woman," she told me. "It crept up on me. I started out like thousands of women, getting a job, assuming I'd keep it for a few years into marriage, then quit to have a family. I got

married at twenty-four, but we wound up disappointing each other and got divorced.

"I still had my job at that time," she continued,
"and it was a slightly *better* job. So I threw myself into
it to offset the pain of a failed marriage. I wanted to
do something right."

Judith worked for a man who was charming and
boyish, and whose greatest gift was diplomacy and
public relations—he could sooth an angry mob. Judith
was raised to be a pleaser—to be accommodating,
acquiescent and adoring—and she did so reluctantly,
to get along in the world. They were a perfect team.
The Soother needed someone to blame his gaffes on,
someone to tell him he was what he wasn't—a great
decision-maker. Judith fulfilled both roles—she "mis-
placed" papers he hadn't actually bothered to complete, bailed him out of problems he'd put off, excusing
himself by saying he was overworked. He gave her
more responsibility as she proved she could handle any
schedule and took the credit for her work. It was 1973
and Judith fought falling in love with him.

"I liked being part of a team," she said. "He needed
me the way my husband never did. I gave him everything I had, every drop of energy, every bit of my
loyalty. He promoted me."

Judith developed a different sense of her work as
she identified more with the job—*it was her.* Work

formed the structure of her life. It was what she chatted about with friends and family. It influenced how she shopped for clothes, shopped for food. She brought work home and woke up excited about getting into her car and going to, not her job, her *life*.

"I lived for my boss," she said. "His attention kept me alive. I couldn't imagine not working. I thought about my mother, and how she treated my father when he came home, dragged out from a factory job. She'd pat him on the back, tell him what was for dinner and listen as he raved on about the injustices at the plant. I didn't want to be her. And I was earning as much as my father was making. I was guilty about it for a while, then I thought, what's the point? Enjoy it."

Judith worked happily alongside her boss for six years, following orders. She'd been in love with him years before, but now things had changed. She was in love with his job. They'd never had an affair—though they'd kissed once, almost to clear the air and dispel the sexual tension between them. They knew it was a mistake to pursue a physical involvement, but in her heart it was unrequited love, not just smart office politics.

Her boss was a clever politician too, but he was not a real threat—laterally or vertically. She wanted his job. She knew how to do it better than he did; she'd been performing it for him to perfection; everyone knew it was Judith who really drove the team. Being sweet insured her job, but now she was changing her definition of goodness. She wanted to be appreciated, but upon closer scrutiny, it wasn't appreciation that kept her at her desk, it was exploitation, and that wasn't good for her.

She wasn't proud of it, but she got her boss fired. It took the better part of a year. Her first step was to let slip her "concern" for the Soother and how his sudden and erratic behavior made it hard for her to work efficiently. He began drinking; she reported it. She reported everything. They rewarded her with his job—for the same salary.

After seven years at the company, with a new title after her name, Judith saw her destiny—the top slot. No one would stand in her way.

She took courses in business to learn everything so she would never be caught short not knowing, doubly humiliated because she was a woman not knowing. It was the 1970s and the male-dominated corporate image was the norm. For Judith, these years were bliss. Planning strategy became her, corporate game-playing put a blush on her cheek, dinner meetings were as exciting as assignations. She dressed in suits and silk shirts, kept her blond hair a bit above shoulder length, and walked with the stride of a hungry spear-throwing hunter pacing his mark.

Judith had a secret—a personal life with few close friends, no lover and a growing number of "sport sex" encounters. Men, she said, didn't find her appealing as a love partner, but they were pleased enough to take her to bed for a night. What was wrong with her? Business fascinated her the way it fascinated men, and she thought it was the trick to bringing them closer. In the dim past when she was "weak, sweet and dumb on cue," men had treated her as if she were the human version of room service. When she achieved, at least she got long-term rewards from the company. She wasn't asked to leave when they were done with her.

Judith came to see me because she couldn't sleep, and when she woke she felt panic and loneliness. "Men don't like me anymore. Do I have to be something I'm not to get a man?"

Judith has set up her life so that ambition comes first. The person who emerged from the corporate battleground has a different set of values, standards and characteristics than the Judith who adored her Soother. Looking to men as role models, she's adopted their ploys and their tactics for getting the competitive edge—being tougher than other women and a challenge to men. Her job is her true love, and her lovers appear temporarily in disconnected encounters. She talks about them as purely carnal outlets, denying her need for affection, human touch, warmth, caring, a chance to be vulnerable with another person. The men are "wrong," but there are no "right" ones out there for her. If she's starved, any nice-enough guy with the right parts will do.

Dr. Srully Blotnick, writing of the private lives of successful career women in his book *Otherwise Engaged,* says of "love 'em and leave 'em" types that "the needs they hoped would vanish had instead been accumulating, disrupting their ability to make important distinctions once men were near. The result was that they wound up becoming involved with men to whom, under ordinary circumstances, they might not have even said hello."

Judith's ambition is her companion, one that doesn't leave her. Its rewards prove her worth as a person, that she's somebody. She focused on ambition and it took her places, but the trip was costly. Installed in her corner office, she's lonely, and to avoid dealing with how empty her life is, she accelerates her pace at work. It's a matter of occupation squelching *pre*occupation. Will the needs vanish?

I think not; Judith agrees.

Judith and Kate are two sides of the unfulfilled career woman. One cannot live without love and chooses to deny that she's a fully developed individual with skills and talent; loneliness terrifies her. Another cannot live *with* love, choosing to deny a need for intimacy; loneliness terrifies her, too. For Kate, a man is everything; Judith *is* the man she wants. At one extreme, there's Kate, the "cream puff," obsessed with love, pyschologically bloated from images of Hal. He's empty calories now, yet Kate gorges on memories, unable to acknowledge how nourishing her accomplishments are. Judith holds down the opposite end—she's the "tart." As if it were a source of shame, Judith masks her true appetite for love—but she snacks on casual sex. Her psychological fuel is work—gluttonous amounts of work. And just the way a binge on a tray of brownies is a narcotic for depression, so work narcotizes Judith— it temporarily numbs feelings, allowing her to carry on. Satiated by sweet, long hours of work, she can fake a casualness about love to fool the world.

Judith's and Kate's stories aren't isolated examples. They're two very poignant demonstrations of what women are going through—trying to solve the quandary of establishing a career while having a noncompetitive love relationship with a man. The balance between the two seems elusive, though it's not. One reason we see no solution is that we feel we *must* make a choice, accepting one and excluding the other. Another influence is our craving for superlatives. We're hypnotized by the glamor of extremes—Supermom. Superstar. Baby moguls. Teen tycoons. Ten Women Who Made Millions Before Thirty. And to be sure we never lose our competitive grip in future years, Marathon Runners Seventy and Over.

Our culture sells us on these lofty images and tells us to strive for them or marry them or be doomed to inadequacy. "The mediocre are always at their best," a French philosopher stated cynically, but that cynicism fairly expresses widely held current views on daring to be average, daring to be *nice*. The wildly exaggerated expectations and unrealistic goals we set for ourselves are bound to disappoint 99 percent of us. Only a few reach the top slot. For many of us, a good job is as good as a great job. It's a matter of being content with *who* you are and *where* you are and acknowledging the compatibility between your deeper nature and its expression in your life. Only a few of us marry the movie star or the corporation chairman. He's not necessarily a better person for having achieved, he just looks better. He has the trappings. Maybe that's enough for you. But if it isn't, then you're better off saying yes to the sweet guys, the ones who'll be there for you and make your life better.

*　　*　　*

A better life is a balanced life. And the only way to have one is to confront the truth about what you need from a man and what you want from your career. Why do you *need* a man? If not for the traditional trade-offs of marriage—identity, belonging, dependency, status—then what? How do you choose men? Has your ambition affected your standards? What do you ask of a career?

Let's take the first step toward creating a balance between love and work and see what may be standing in the way.

The following questions will help you clarify the direction your life is taking. You'll see if you're moving toward a balance between work and love, or if you've created a "seesaw" effect, with love weighing down one end while productive work is teetering or flailing in midair, or the reverse, giving too much weight to work while love—the "lightweight" among your priorities—is suspended.

These questions are divided into two categories: relationships and work. They'll ask you to examine your attitudes, feelings, values and approaches. You'll see a pattern begin to emerge as you go through the questions, and you may see where you need to make adjustments.

*   *   *

Relationships: Men, Friends, Family and Children

1. Is my social life slipping away?

2. Do I fear a relationship with a man because he might convince me to give up the work I love?

3. Do I put off relationships with men because I spend too much time worrying about pleasing them and not enough on my work?

4. Do I discount the importance of men in the lives of my friends?

5. Do I mock my friends when they express a desire to have a husband and family?

6. Is it easier for me to have one-night stands as I get older?

7. Have I given up on love and settled for a sex life?

8. Do I think I'm "above" love—that it has nothing to do with me, is just for others?

9. Do I frequent restaurants, resorts and so forth where there are fewer men than women, proving there are "no" men?

10. Must the man I want be special, not average, for me to know I've achieved in my social life as well as in my professional life?

11. Am I content visiting with a sibling's (or friend's) children—happy to be "Auntie," never "Mom"?

12. Does a preoccupation with pets, shopping, cleaning, overeating *and* working cover a deeper need to connect with a man?

13. Now that I have a career, do I find myself bored in the company of full-time homemakers?

14. Do I feel women complain too much about their children, their husbands, their inability to make a decision about what to do in life?

15. Do I see the average woman as inferior, taking an elitist position toward women who aren't ambitious?

16. Have I ended friendships because I couldn't tolerate friends getting ahead?

17. Have friends backed out of relationships with me because my success threatens them? Did I let them go easily?

18. Do I want friends to treat me with a certain deference now that I'm successful, and to understand why things must be done according to my schedule?

19. Am I becoming more distant and less accessible to friends, lovers, family?

20. Do I feel angry or unhappy much of the day, without being able to pinpoint the problem exactly?

21. Can I have an exciting day at the office but feel depressed or angry as bedtime approaches and I'm alone?

22. Do I think that men who make less money than I do are totally ineligible to fit into my life?

23. Do I worry about my professional image—preferring to go to a function alone rather than with a man whom others may not consider "suitable"?

24. Do I feel humiliated when I'm placed in the position of serving others, even if it's just a casual get-together at which I'm *asked* to get the ice cubes, start the coffee maker, and so forth?

25. Do I feel demeaned and angry if someone forgets my position and introduces me as "Bob's girlfriend" (or wife or sister) or describes me as having a lower-level position than I do?

26. If a man calls me "girl," do I respond with hostility, although, in fact, I may often call female friends "you guys" or, in spite of myself, "girls"?

27. Does the man in my life know what I want and is he generally supportive?

28. Do I get distracted listening to my husband's (boyfriend's) problems, and anxiously wait to talk about mine?

29. Am I no longer supportive of a man's goals? Do I try to redirect him toward what I think is a better idea?

30. Is it hard for me to tell people I like them or compliment them when they've done something good?

31. Do I feel embarrassed when men are vulnerable, mistaking it for weakness?

32. Do I respect other people's feelings but find that sometimes it's impossible to be caring?

33. If I ask for support from a man and he responds in a way that's clumsy or inappropriate, do I become angry and want to strike back?

34. Do I feel competition with my siblings in spite of myself and find it impossible to control snide comments about their triumphs, great or small?

35. Do I like telling people how much I do for others?

36. Am I confused about what I need from others emotionally?

37. When I ask for emotional support from a man, do I somehow feel overly sensitive, depressed or worried that he will take advantage of me?

Work: Fantasies, Ambitions, Goals and Attitudes

1. Do I find my greatest pleasure is in work?

2. If my work goes well, does that mean more to me than if I'm having a comfortable relationship with a man?

3. Am I caught up in what an executive career woman is supposed to look like—overly tailored, female, but not too "feminine"?

4. If I dress in the corporate image, am I comfortable with it?

5. Am I interested in having an affair with my boss or any officer in the company because I believe that sex buys power?

6. Am I critical of coworkers if I feel they've moved ahead of me?

7. Will I put my name on someone else's work?

8. Am I willing to forge ahead or succeed at any price?

9. Do I feel I'm in competition with every man and woman in the office?

10. Do I get to work an hour early and leave two, three or four hours after five o'clock because I feel I must prove myself?

11. Have I given a lot of thought to office politics, and do I agree they're necessary for survival there?

12. Have I come to think of the people I work with as my "real" family, instead of my blood relatives and friends I've made over the years?

13. Do I find myself influenced by trends, including the idea of "having it all"?

14. Do I feel that it's not enough that I succeed, but that others must fail?

15. Do I feel that I have to undermine others' work just enough to make them feel doubt or strip them of glory?

16. Do I have a proprietary attitude about the office in general—guarding files, equipment, charts, stationery, inventory, as if it were all my own?

17. Do I want to become famous to prove to others that I can be somebody?

18. Have I become a master at game-playing in the office—worrying that if I don't, others will outmaneuver me?

19. Do I feel guilty if I spend a day that doesn't involve work or work-related social events?

20. Do I really love my career, or is it just a readily available companion, one I can call on any time of the day or night?

21. Do I *want* to believe that people get ahead because they're competent, loyal, hard-working and nice to be around, without really believing that's true at all?

22. Do I thrive on high-pressure jobs?

23. Do I fear retirement?

24. Am I preoccupied with money—what I earn and how to make more, what others earn?

25. Do I have an unexplained sense of urgency about my professional life—as if I had to get somewhere before a certain date?

Were most of your answers to these questions *yes?* If so, the source of your problem may be that you've unplugged your basic nature and tuned in to a more "male-oriented" style of living. By design or default, you've compartmentalized love and work, as many achieving men do, and you're feeling the stress of a life out of control. Ambition thrives for you, love withers. You want to be strong, but forget that it is equally important to be vulnerable—to let it happen.

On the road to liberation and self-fulfillment, women may have overcome the fear of success and the fear of failure, but in place of these two classic disorders, we've developed another—the fear of vulnerability. Love cannot exist without vulnerability—a willingness to surrender to love, feel trust in a man, safety, peace. The vulnerable rarely rule. The ambitious personality saves his or her fragile side for the very few, fearing that a show of compliance or need will precede a fall from power.

Thus, today's career woman has toughened up. Her involvement with work seems to have trained her to neglect her softer side—to empathize, to be more accepting of human failings (hers and those of others she loves), to nurture, extend herself generously. Male-style office strategies have transplanted themselves from office to home, and in many cases set up competition between men and women.

We're not sure what's *feminine,* and if we are, we worry that we'll have to give up some of the gains we have made. Let's see what's confusing us about "femininity" now.

Femininity Then and Now

"The essential nature of femininity is unknown except to women, who are neither interested in it nor willing to enlighten us men about it," wrote a very cynical and baffled Dr. Theodore Reik in his book *The Need To Be Loved*. Twenty years ago, when it was written, we'd have agreed with this statement. Yes, we women are reticent and enigmatic beings and it's just such mystery that beguiles men. The essential nature of femininity is *secrecy*. Then, we believed it was our power.

The definition of feminine was fairly universal then: dependent, passive, acquiescent, agreeable, pretty, courageous within the family, curvy, nurturing, instructive, sacrificing, ambitious for one's spouse, obedient, sexually initiated by the man one marries. For a woman to be "feminine" then, she had to attract a male. The reason was obvious: marriage, family and economic survival. Men had dominion over what *was* feminine (women) and what wasn't (strength, adventurousness, aggression, logical thinking) . . . you get the point.

The 1950s American woman who adhered to the "feminine" format could be transplanted anywhere in the world and socialize without raising eyebrows. She would, first of all, defer to males and instinctively let them know it by gesture and tone of voice. Men would respond as *they* had been taught—pull out her chair, hold the door, light her cigarette, apologize for profanity in her company, flatter her and inquire about her children, mother and husband or simply ignore her. Life was easier when everyone *agreed* about how people should behave.

The qualities described as feminine then aren't bad in themselves, but they were restricted to one sex and packaged so that to be "feminine" meant being mindless, without a will, without a sense of purpose, a cliché of manners and morals.

Then the women's movement marched through the gender gap, and the dust is still rising. For a while, as women sought to redefine who they were and where they wanted to be, the definition of "femininity" was uncertain. We tried to sort out which quality belonged to whom and why. Biology determines how our bodies are formed, but gender identity, or sex roles, determine how we *behave*. Women pattern themselves consciously and unconsciously after their mothers and pick up a few qualities from their fathers. This patterning begins when we're very young. Parents remind us of what girls do and what boys do, and so do teachers, friends, even novels, films and fashion.

Feminism didn't ask that we subscribe to gender blending—becoming androgynous—but that women stop limiting themselves to narrow definitions of male and female, femininity and masculinity. It told us that women didn't have to be only mothers, wives and daughters, economically beholden to a husband or father. We didn't have to be patronized when we had insights, ideas, plans that extended beyond the front door or discouraged or humiliated when we talked of fulfilling work for ourselves. As opportunity beyond the home became a realistic choice, as we began reaching for goals formerly only achieved by men, "femininity" took on different shadings. It became grayer for some, brighter for others.

Work. Of all our recent strides, none is as great as how we've changed because of productive work. It's contributed more to our redefinition of ourselves than anything else. Years ago, women worked largely in support positions—secretaries, nurses, domestics, kitchen help, teachers—and no one accused them of being unfeminine. Hollywood actresses weren't quite considered "career women," since they were most often controlled by teams of men—agents, managers, directors, studio heads. To be fully eligible for "femininity" and hold a job, a woman had to keep her peace and not challenge a male domain. And because femininity included the trait of order-taking, not order-giving, women were often summarily dismissed as being incapable of success in business.

But were we?

Women weren't prepared to compete in the business world. We were trained to compete with one another for the most desirable men. We weren't prepared to succeed in business, but to meet the goals and obligations of marriage and find success at home. Women were prepared to fail. The new feminism argued: We have minds, aspirations, energy, courage and talent, and the world is full of opportunity. We didn't need to fail any longer, but we didn't know how to succeed. Qualities that previously brought us rewards—dependency, obedience—were now considered liabilities in the work world. If nice guys finished last, what chance would a compliant woman have out there? We needed to toughen up to fit into the world men had built.

Men showed us what to do often in spite of themselves. Few men willingly give up power, or voluntarily offer their vulnerable spots, especially when history and economics have always been in their favor, but we were out to change history. We took careful notes on board-room behavior and everything that men did at work. Pull back here, press forward there. Assert. Demand. Keep your enemies off balance. Join teams, run teams. Finesse. Rethink communication. Learn diplomacy without tears. Jungle fight if you've got the fever. And win.

Although we toughened up at work, at home we still wanted love, a good relationship. But times had changed, we'd changed and many men stayed the same. Many now accept a woman's place in the work force, but they hope for a "feminine" woman at home— someone with whom they can be vulnerable, who doesn't compete with them, who doesn't demand that he cook dinner when it's "his turn." Somewhere in these last years of growth for women, we looked to male behavior patterns for instruction on how to further our careers and sacrificed a part of ourselves.

Femininity is the best of who we are—nurturing, vulnerable, comforting, seeing humor in an otherwise grim situation and making it easier for others, telling others we love them and deriving pleasure from that. Femininity has also grown to mean self-assurance, independence and ambition. Feminine women *do* compete, but they don't have to give up their personal lives or their basic natures to get on in this world.

How We've Gone From Cream Puff to Tart— The Male Traits that Tempted Us, then Trapped Us

We live in a world built by men and no one knows this better than a woman with ambitions. If she is going to make it, she knows she must be astute, courageous, a taker of risks, willing to play the games men invented for themselves, secret signals and all. The ambitious woman wants to *net* the power, not nest with it, never mind how she was raised. Perhaps history didn't prepare her for authority in the work place, and biology didn't endow her with testosterone, but emotionally she considers herself ready to compete and win.

Men taught her how.

Some women learned male-image behavior so well that they found themselves embroiled in similar lifestyle crises and health-related problems. Relationships suffered as women invested much of their energy in mapping out careers, *then marrying them.*

This situation mirrored the life of her male counterpart, whose marriage to jobs created a strained home life with a bitter wife and overindulged children who compensated with "things" because he was away so much of the time. There are a few differences: Workaholism is more socially acceptable for men than for women. A man can maintain distance from intimate relationships and still be thought of as a man. To work is good, to work hard is better, to work hardest is a tribute. This is not true for women. If a woman is disconnected from intimate relationships, she often goes through greater torment, even if she's running a major corporation. Emotional distancing helped her climb to the top. She has confused the gratification of a job with the emotional gratification of a personal life—rejecting the one in which she is vulnerable in favor of the other, in which she's safe and calling the shots.

Love and work do battle for many ambitious women. Somehow, in figuring out and conquering male power systems, they forgot about feelings, progressively building disdain for intimacy and sensitivity. Some may have declined marriage, thinking it was a "trap," but they are just as confined in the marriage they've made with their occupation, and they may just be realizing that now.

The striving woman *does* work hard. She'll happily relate stories of the sacrifices she's made to reach her goal and how she's paid her dues. Some of those dues were paid with overwork and neglect of love relationships—two traits borrowed, unconsciously or consciously, directly from her hand-picked male mentors or role models, the men who taught her much of what she knows about navigating her way down the fast track.

Let's look at them one at a time.

Workaholism: In her book *Leaving the Office Behind,* psychologist Barbara Mackoff studied the growing problem of overinvolvement with work, to the exclusion and detriment of relationships, a comfortable family life and restorative time to let one's mind and body recover from daily stress, long hours and haphazard eating patterns. She made a wonderful point and expressed it in a way that sounds almost proverbial: No one lies on his or her deathbed wishing he or she had spent more time at the office.

Workaholics work and look for more work to fill gaps in their lives as they occur. Mackoff says that many workaholics see their efforts as "dedication," not overwork. Whatever noble reason they assign to their productivity, workaholics really get the kind of emotional gratification from work they may not get from relationships. And so they work—to prove they are worthy human beings, to assuage feelings of loneliness by filling the time with constructive activity instead of doing nothing and bemoaning their fate. Time flies when one is occupied, and no one understands that more than the workaholic woman. Industriousness consumes her life, and unless she finds a male workaholic whose pattern is compatible with hers, her preoccupation with keeping busy may hurt her.

Dr. Meyer Friedman wrote a landmark book, *Type A Behavior and Your Heart,* on dynamic men, driven individuals who shared what he called "Type A" behavior. These men were ambitious and successful, but they also had heart problems. Some women are classified as Type A, too, and like their male counterparts, they are compelled to overwork by a driving ambition and are undone by the professional pressures. Both male and female Type A's have low self-esteem, fear that they weren't loved by the opposite-sex parent when they were children and need constant attention and recognition to feel worthy. Though all their energy goes into work, they suffer from a sad and self-sabotaging inability to be tender—to themselves and often to others.

The ambitious woman should be praised for the strength, fortitude, imagination, guts and energy she pours into productive work, but she should be alerted to what she's losing by denying the need for a balance between love and work. Or sadder yet, denying the need for a relationship at all.

Saying No to Love: Yes, it's true: intimate relationships *do* restrict your freedom, because your thoughts and activities are affected by another person's life in addition to your own. Therefore, some ambitious women have said no to love—forgetting that a loving relationship is not *all* restriction, but involves freedom too. With mutual caring, there's a freeing of the *spirit* that puts your failures, mistakes and shortcomings in a different perspective. It's the same spirit that *accepts* who you are, too.

Ambitious men have a legendary inability to maintain a balance between their personal and professional lives, and the ambitious woman thrusting herself forward on the straight and narrow course toward success is following suit. One key belief, beyond the fear that preoccupation with a man is a distraction, is that intimacy is *life*-consuming. They prefer expending energy on productive work to the exclusion of productive love. The reasons go deeper, and intimacy may suffer because these women fear control and male influence.

"I was raised to serve men," a forty-seven-year-old woman in the environmental movement tells me, "and if I get involved in a relationship, I know myself—I glaze over, go numb and give myself over to the guy and forget what I want to accomplish at work. All I want now is some male attention on occasion—and let them go home after sex."

"I've taken a twenty-seven-year-old lover," a forty-year-old woman vice-president of a major corporation admits. "He's my 'dumb blond' and you know what he's good for—dinner and sex a few times a week. I don't want to know any more about him."

For these women who choose casual sex over intimacy, detachment proves how strong they are, how great their mission is, how cleverly detached they are from the men used for comfort and pleasure, even how radically liberated they are by proclaiming contempt for the very men they could truly care for. But what matters most of all to them is that a man cannot control them, or have any emotional influence on them at all.

Ambitious women who are determined to show the world they are "good enough," worthy of attention and high regard, have tight reins on their careers. They are practiced at controlling themselves and others at work, and that lack of vulnerability slowly transfers itself to their personal lives. They fear that intimacy is tantamount to a *loss* of control, that it will bring on disrespect and abuse. As with the men after whom they pattern themselves, emotional isolation and sport sex make them feel *safe*. They need people, but loathe that part of themselves. They've made a virtue of a lack of affection—yearning for *something,* but denying that it is tenderness. They want it all—but on their own terms.

Having It All: The Spoiler

One of the most electrifying moments in history brought Geraldine Ferraro to the podium to accept the vice-presidential nomination in the 1984 presidential election. Whether you found her personally appealing or not, whether you found her qualified for the office or not, she stood before us as a symbol of achievement and *possibility* for other women. She "had it all" and was on the threshold of having more.

Married for about twenty-five years at that time, the mother of three children, a law school graduate, congressional representative from her district in Queens, New York, Geraldine Ferraro possessed a commodity that became much coveted in the 1980s—that *balance* between personal life and career, proving that love and occupation were not mutually exclusive. The "Queens housewife" had it all for everyone to see—a still-affectionate long-term marriage, bright children, a career rewarded by recognition and achievement, a nice apartment, a loyal hairdresser and even a sympathetically poignant upbringing by a widowed working-class mother.

Having it all suited Geraldine Ferraro very well, very *naturally*.

"I have sacrificed everything in my life that I consider precious in order to advance the political career of my husband," said her opposite, Pat Nixon. Today, we can feel vividly the melancholy in her voice, the *fatigue* of having given one's life to the service of another. Pat Nixon was a shy woman who did her duty, spent an astonishing life in spite of herself, and actually cast a vote for career wives (along with Nancy Reagan) by giving them a new credibility—it was okay to be a diligent support system to an ambitious husband. We may not identify with Pat Nixon, we may not want to trade places with her, but we acknowledge that she and her husband make a good all-American *team*.

Geraldine Ferraro did something else—she reinspired women who had a dream.

She had it all, and she'd had it for *decades*. How did she do it? Luck? The good sense to know what was right for her, and who was right for her, and then go for it? Was her success a matter of destiny? Planning? Toughness?

How did she do it? women asked as she stood there at that podium, and how can I? The ambitious woman asking this question saw in Ferraro an ideal—*an accessible ideal*. She was us, in a way. The kind of person we'd have gone to school with, done our nails with, cried with, campaigned for. We knew her, identified with her, liked her guts in speaking her mind in that broad New York accent.

Having it all never looked so delectable as when it was served by its reigning mistress, Geraldine Ferraro. The "have-it-all package" had been forced down our throats during the five-year period before the 1984 election. It promised that along with achievement at work, we could have marriage to men who accepted our careers. We'd have children, work as a team toward some goal, reach prosperity . . . then have it all.

Three things happened: Ferraro's ticket lost, her husband, John Zaccaro, found himself in financial difficulty and their only son was arrested, charged with drug dealing on a college campus. If this was having it all, some woman said, "I'd rather punch a switchboard." The lights went off for Ferraro—our ideal was shot down. She was not only married to a man whose ethics we secretly wondered about, but she might have failed as a mother. We could rationalize away her husband's complicated money problems, but not her son, a druggie, who reflected on *her*. She was on the stump while her son was on cocaine and selling it. Where were the boy's standards? Why didn't his mother take care of him before such public humiliation?

Many women abandoned Ferraro—spiritually and politically. No longer the ideal, no longer a symbol of having it all, she was once again a Queens housewife, with the same family crises as thousands of other mothers across America. We wanted more from her and she disappointed us.

It's sad for Ferraro, and sad for us too, that many of us now diminish her accomplishments because of her family's problems. Or, maybe it's because she's proved a fear that bubbles just below the surface—dare to go for it all and punishment will follow on the heels of success. We should allow Ferraro her success and applaud it, not use her setbacks as excuses to stop striving. Don't fall into the trap of competing cruelly with other women—pouncing on Ferraro after the fall, and on other women we know personally who rise and fall as we look on.

Having it all *is* delectable, and you needn't try for it on so grand a scale as achieving lofty public office for it to matter. A lesser version is equally rewarding and fulfilling, and less trying on the nerves. It's one that allows you to live within your own limits, not measure yourself against lofty standards set by unique individuals. If you have productive work that you like and that suits you—not a career title that sounds good involving work you dislike—and productive love, you have the basis for a warm, loving life. You, my friend, have it all!

Men prove themselves to men, women prove themselves to men and sisterhood is not perfect. This is a truth of the 1980s. We've gone far, but we've gotten lost within all these complicated interrelationships merely trying to please everyone, including ourselves. We must sit back, relax and take a hard look at who we are, what we want; if it's a loving relationship with a man who, realistically, should he be? In a career, where are we headed? What efforts can we make to keep the two working together?

The greatest misfortune occurs when a woman sacrifices her personal life to get ahead. Investing in marriage and family is as valuable as pursuing a career. The greatest kindness any woman can offer herself is to not depreciate intimacy and love and let herself be dazzled by power. The greatest favor a woman can give herself is to find what she likes to do, concentrate on doing it well and let her career unfold at a steady pace. Work has no sex. Don't step out there to prove that you're as good as anyone—ready to destroy yourself and the very thing you hunger for: balance in love and work.

Life is miraculous. If you live it in a balance of love and work, you'll reach "that certain age" with no regrets.

6

Finally . . . No Regrets

I'LL put it to you this way," Betty said. "Tony has no equal. Giving him up is giving up everything. I'll never find anyone like him again, not at this point in my life." Betty's sitting in my office testing her resistance to smoking by clutching an unopened pack of cigarettes. To mark a nineteen-year relationship with a man who will not fully commit to her, Betty's decided to give up smoking. Her other addiction, Tony, will be the more difficult and painful one to surrender.

Betty's here to see me so she can come to terms with Tony as he is. She can't leave him, not yet, but she is terribly frustrated by the conditions of the relationship. Betty's been "living with" Tony on weekends for the last seventeen years. She travels to his house on Friday night and leaves Monday morning for work at a nearby hospital where she's an operating-room nurse. She loves Tony for his uniqueness—he's interesting, handsome, athletic, a self-made man; he speaks three languages fluently, and while he's not especially witty, he *can* carry a tune. When he's in a good mood, he's extravagantly generous. He's fifty-four years old, veteran of a marriage that lasted one summer, thirty-two years ago.

Betty met Tony twenty years ago after her divorce. They fell in love. "Tony calls the shots," Betty tells me. "Four years ago, I got up the courage and began putting pressure on him to get married. We had been dating fifteen years! Was I wrong? He said I was nagging him, and that he'd get married when he was ready and not sooner. I pushed some more and he disappeared for four months—he wouldn't take my calls or answer the door when I knew he was home. I went to his office and his secretaries protected him like armed guards.

"Tony called me when he wanted to come back," she continued, "and picked up the conversation as if nothing had happened." The conversation told the story of their relationship. Betty asked why he hadn't called and he replied he had been busy. "I didn't ask him where he'd been," Betty said. "He trained me well. I actually believed it wasn't my business."

Betty will celebrate her fiftieth birthday this year, including twenty years spent with this paragon among Junk Food Heroes. What does she have? Two decades of her life have been invested in a man to whom real intimacy and loving are unknown. He cannot commit to Betty, will not consider living together full-time or marriage. Living together gives Betty complete access to him and marriage, in his mind, gives her what she wants, so he'll do neither. He's in control, and he's been in control for twenty years. Betty's given him no reason to change—she'll do what he wants whether he bullies her or vanishes from her life.

"If I leave Tony," she says in a small voice, "I'll be alone. The thought of losing him completely panics me. I want to know how to accept this arrangement, even if it's for the rest of my life, and not feel cheated."

When I listen to Betty speak of Tony, I hear the despair of unfulfilled love. I hear the words of all women like her who have not yet made the distinction between real love and addictive love—junk food love. They're women who valiantly say that they're trying to have no regrets having loved the men they've known, but they regret not having loved themselves too.

For women suffering from low self-esteem, the word "love" has a remarkably persuasive quality, particularly when it is accompanied by the usual tag line: "If you love me, you'll have another drink with me . . . have sex in a way you don't like . . . do as I say because I know what's best for you . . . stop seeing your friends," even "kill for me." When you are addicted to junk food love, it has a hold on you. Sit quietly in a room and think about your Junk Food lover, and chances are you will begin to feel an odd, gnawing *pain*—a craving, even a flash of panic. A psychological dependency has taken over—you think the craving is greater than the person causing the addiction and stronger than your ability to control it.

Not so!

Addiction goes through its own mean cycle. There's the addictive substance—for example, the Junk Food lover, whether he's a Shark, a Boss, a Golden Boy, a Blaster or another type—slick, authoritative to the point of suffocation, a narcissist, an underdog with violent tendencies. Whoever he is, he gives you what you want at first. He provides pleasure, intensity and a false sense of security. Because you're lulled by a temporary and blissful comfort, he hooks you. With the addiction comes your belief that Junk Food lovers supply you with sustenance, strength and confidence—not that you have your own ego and emotional resources.

The addiction takes on such inflated importance that

you are weakened by the thought of separation or loss. This is the second stage of the cycle. One hallmark of addictive love is that to the "user," separation from the substance is an intolerable prospect. When you can't let go of junk food love, you prefer the pain of overdosing—staying with a man for more of the same unwholesome way of life he feeds you—rather than breaking the connection, enduring a temporarily painful withdrawal period, and then recovering, free from the craving! The threat of loss brings up such anxiety that you'll do almost anything to maintain the relationship. If it means forgoing a normal life to sustain the addiction, so be it.

As the momentum gathers, addiction to junk food love undermines self-confidence and interferes with your ability to make decisions or feel free to take any independent action. The primary reason for disentangling yourself from the relationship is the same reason you stay: You feel entrapped by the man. He's your obsession, your drug. He's no good for you, and you're in conflict over whether "no good" is good enough or not.

There's a checklist of symptoms that go with such addictiveness—all of them pointing to low self-esteem:

• Even if you're an intelligent, usually rational and functioning individual, you are hopelessly responsive to any suggestion that you are inadequate. Your Junk Food Hero is happy to make the suggestion.

• You have a fear of complete independence and believe you couldn't make it in the world without an anchor, a protector, a guardian, an authority. With such low self-confidence, it's hard to leave the man to whom you've turned over the power to run your life.

• Because you are afraid of independence, you seek out a man who'll become the focus of your life and make him your addiction. Before long, you feel that only constant exposure to him makes life bearable. Eventually, though, life becomes *un*bearable for you. Constant exposure wears you down.

• You discover that junk food love is toxic to your spirit, and it can affect you physically, too. You are often tired, but don't know why.

Women are especially prone to addictive love, if only because of the role traditionally mapped out for us. We've been raised to believe that *helplessness* is a virtue, and to accept rewards for being incapacitated. But if we are helpless we have no way to experience life for ourselves and we become insulated in our little worlds. Once there, we are locked into narrow ideals, looking no further than the immediate neighborhoods of our lives, distrusting outsiders and new ideas. Any woman who grows up fearful will always give too much credence to other people's opinions. She'll be awed by authority and look to junk food love as the single solution to the question, Who am I?

If women could seek love out of strength, not weakness, from faith in ourselves, not out of a need to worship another, they'd recognize who the good men are and who they are *not*. Good men are willing to grow. Junk Food Heroes crave unconditional love—they want to be unchallenged and accepted with all their flaws. They're less likely to make compromises to accommodate you, but they are quick to point out your flaws and how you must accommodate *them*.

"This isn't good enough for me." Learn to say this statement for yourself, with no apologies, no hysteria, no fear. A good man will listen and make an effort to improve the relationship. If you do not ask for what you need, you may go through life settling for the crumbs, empowering men to control you and asking them to fulfill your ambitions. If you'd rather live with a man who mistreats you than live alone, you'll spend your life under a man's thumb and regret it! Here are the steps you can take toward ending your addiction to junk food love and finding the right man.

* * *

Going Cold Turkey

Detoxifying from the wrong kind of love and building self-esteem isn't a simple overnight process. You need time for a daily renewal of determination and persistence. Your self-respect will increase day by day and you will begin to see changes in how you perceive yourself and the world. Remember: You must be healthy to recognize a sweet man and healthy enough to accept him into your life!

Let's start by asking a question you must answer honestly.

1. Who's to blame? Know who you are and don't blame others for your own flaws. There's nothing you can do about the past—it's irretrievable and it's over. Obsession with what you've missed reinforces feelings of worthlessness. Stop yourself every time you feel the despair or anger connected with what was, and substitute a one-sentence attitude or goal phrased positively to move you out of the past and into your future. Today, the past is done. *I am lovable. I am capable. I am able to accomplish the tasks I set for myself.* Forget the word "not."

2. Next, examine your life in detail. Try to pick out your psychological connections to the junk food loves of your life, then write your own autobiography. You'll do best if you don't fudge information or squelch feelings that seem unacceptable to you. Face the truth. *Forgive yourself.* The only way to recover from debilitating situations is to recognize the bad feelings they produce and how they affect you negatively. Detach from your old self—the one that feels like someone you used to be, but are no more. Give "her" a pet name, if you like. But visualize her as part of your past.

3. Clarify your values and what you want out of a relationship. Does the relationship you have *now* live up to those goals or have the potential to allow you to reach them? What obstacles do you see? Is it clear to you that there is no such thing as a perfect relationship and that you must work at a relationship every day? Relationships ebb and flow and so will yours.

4. Distance yourself from a person you crave in an unhealthy way. Stay with friends or get an answering machine so you don't have to speak to him by phone, but be sure to give yourself a week away from the relationship. Pretend you're out of town and phones aren't available. Think it out. Instead of counting up his transgressions against you and lamenting about what you should have done, figure out how to feel good about yourself. Take this time to build emotional stam-

ina to defuse the Junk Food Hero's power over you.
If you feel a desperate need to call him, wait ten
minutes. If you still feel the tug, wait another ten, then
twenty more. Keep lengthening the waiting time. If
you must call, promise yourself that if he says something negative, you will thank him for taking the call
and hang up. Don't listen or beg for understanding.
Preserve your dignity.

5. Recognize that every woman has unfulfilled
yearnings in her life, whether they involve the quality
or the quantity of love she desires. Life doesn't begin
and end with the heartbeat of a Junk Food Hero. And
giving up junk food love leaves room for many people
and causes far worthier of our time and attention.

6. Give yourself time alone. Being alone does not
mean being isolated and it is not a permanent condition
if you don't choose that it be so. When you're alone
you can explore creativity or just sit and think *pro-
ductively*. Ask yourself if you crave junk food love just
to fill the lonely spaces and create diversions so you
don't have to face yourself as you are.

7. Forgive yourself for what was and go on to what
will be. Addictions have a way of speaking to you with
small but potent voices, reminding you of your shortcomings and weaknesses. Turn those voices off! Get
used to living without them. When the voice says,

"You need him," say out loud, "No, I don't."

8. Concentrate on changing yourself and your responses rather than trying to force your Junk Food Hero to be someone he isn't. You must do the changing and the growing, and it's not up to you to change him. When you alter your responses to him, the nature of the relationship will shift automatically, in spite of what he does or doesn't do.

Your life is *yours* to create and reinvent—and to share with someone you care for. That sharing is the least you should expect and the *most* you should ask of yourself. Your life is a miracle. Addictions make you doubt it. Take these steps one at a time—they're essential if you're going to break addictive behavior. Be aware of why the addiction is occurring and how it occurs, then commit to change. Act bravely and you'll be your own heroine.

How We Change: The Good News

Of all the many expressions of self-doubt, psychologists probably hear "I can't change" more than any other. We cling fervently to this belief because change seems threatening. Of course change is possible, though our minds prevent us from changing too radically too quickly. This is basic human nature at work—we in-sure our *survival* by not changing our minds indiscrim-inately and thereby confusing ourselves. If we could be swayed from one ideology to the next, from one person to the next just by another's suggestion, we'd wander from one thing to the next, never knowing who we really are, who we really love, which religion we really believe in, and so on. Change can put us at risk when we accept it mindlessly, and our decisions become meaningless. But carefully considered changes in our lives can build a new world that's more mean-ingful than we can possibly imagine—the world we choose through the *will* to improve our lives.

The Biggest Challenge For Women

Perhaps the biggest change for women and the most difficult is the change in the definition of love. It seems for all of history we have permitted people to feed us non-nutritious diets, even with a silver spoon. While starving us they have said, "This is love, what I am giving you is love. I restrict you because I love you. I know what you need better than you know yourself. I will make your decisions for you. I will show you what to wear and, ultimately, I will decide how far you can go and what you can achieve in your own life."

The pity of it is that as women we have bought the entire package and have always looked to men, thinking that even though they might be the same age we are, have the same education, the same intelligence, they know more about who we are, what we need and how our lives should be lived. In fact, we thought that they knew the ultimate definition of love and that even if we were hurt by their definition, they were correct and we were not. Thus, not wanting to further hurt ourselves, we accepted their definition. In our acceptance of the myth of their natural superiority, we stunted their growth and our own.

One of the really solid things about women is that we have been forced to change, like it or not, because from early childhood we have sought the approval of others. If others did not like the way we behaved, we changed our behavior. As a result, we were fairly flexible, taking on an enormous array of roles in order to meet the variety of expectations that others had of us. We had the role of daughter and a fixed set of behaviors that went with it, the role of wife and the behaviors that went with that, the role of mother and so forth. And in a variety of environments we acted obedient and respectful and behaved in the socially acceptable ways. Too often the men in our lives were permitted to say, "I am who I am, and I am the same person in all environments. Don't expect anything different of me," and we accepted that.

It is the acceptance of substandard behavior that has permitted women to get into so much difficulty in what I have called junk food love. There is nothing as satisfying and as beautiful as real love. It is a true partnership based on friendship and respect, with an erotic quality that makes you tingle and excited just by thinking of it. And healthy love does not make you feel sick or desperate or obsessed. It does not make you unproductive and angry and weak. Healthy love adds to your feelings of being alive and joyful. It has contained within it the recognition that just as not all marriages end in love, not all love ends in marriage, but that it was a worthwhile experience regardless of the ending.

The other day on the *Phil Donahue Show,* Dr. Charles Garner, professor of psychiatry at Columbia University, told of how he had rewritten the fairy tales that we all heard when we were children. He changed Cinderella to Cindermelda, and in the story relates that the prince had to go away for a time, and while he was gone Cindermelda discovered that she didn't really miss him. In fact, she was just fine. She rethought the relationship and decided that perhaps they had different values and their life together might not really be as good as she had once thought. When the prince came back she said to him, "You know, this has been a wonderful experience and I've learned a lot of things. I've learned how to sew and I can now use that skill to open a dress shop and be able to be financially independent. It's been a good relationship and I thank you for all that you've done for me, but I think we should go our separate ways." The prince agreed. And so Cindermelda opened her dress shop and found somebody who was much more suited to her, and they lived together, working on their relationship for the rest of their days.

Now, I thought that was a rather nice story and frankly, I was shocked when the audience thought it was just terrible. What about the childhood fantasies, the audience protested. Why not tell a little girl that when she grows up her prince will come and transform her and remove her from the environment in which she is being mistreated, elevating her to the position of princess. My sense was that a lot of women in the audience were still waiting for their princes to come. Even if they had been married for twenty years, no man was good enough; or all men were too good—it didn't matter. They hung on to their hope—someday their prince would come and rescue them. And if they couldn't have a prince, maybe their daughters could.

Unfortunately, too many of us still hold on to fairy tales. The best way not to regret love is to recognize it for what it is and to deal with it in a more reality-oriented way. Don't worry, the romance won't go away. You will just be allowed to think about yourself and what's good for you. Stop looking for transformations from others and transform yourself. There's a wonderful saying that the women who sit and wait for the prince typically end by cleaning up after his horse. To have no regrets from this day forward, cut your losses early, if you recognize that you're involved with a Junk Food lover and connected to a man who's not giving you your minimum adult daily requirements of nurturing.

The way to have no regrets is to ask yourself daily, "Is this relationship good for me? Am I getting something out of it, too? What is it that I'm getting out of it? Am I willing to settle for that?"

The way to have no regrets is to say, "There is no one man in the world for me. In fact, the more I make of myself, the less I need from a man and, therefore, the more men are available and the fewer unrealistic expectations I will have."

Love requires time, shared experiences, a bond between two people or the interest in developing one. It means scaling down desires that the other person cannot satisfy, leaving you hungry for love and addicted to scraps. A healthy relationship isn't clung to out of fear or desperation. It's held together with tenderness and the freedom to be the best that you can be. The sweet guys allow it to happen. Why not let it happen to you?

If you have found *A Hero Is More Than Just a Sandwich* to be helpful and informative, and would like to consider taking a seminar with Dr. Friedman—or if you would simply care to share your response to *A Hero Is More Than Just a Sandwich* with Dr. Friedman—please feel free to write to her at the following address:

Dr. Sonya Friedman
111 South Woodward Avenue
Suite 250
Birmingham, Michigan 48011